FINDING HAPPINESS

More in the Classic Wisdom for Modern Minds
series from Macmillan Collector's Library

Falling in Love

Leaving Home

Living Peacefully

FINDING HAPPINESS

Selection and introduction by Zachary Seager

MACMILLAN COLLECTOR'S LIBRARY

This collection first published 2025 by Macmillan Collector's Library
an imprint of Pan Macmillan
The Smithson, 6 Briset Street, London EC1M 5NR
EU representative: Macmillan Publishers Ireland Ltd,
1st Floor, The Liffey Trust Centre, 117–126 Sheriff Street Upper,
Dublin 1, D01 YC43
Associated companies throughout the world
www.panmacmillan.com

ISBN 978-1-0350-4571-6

Introduction copyright © Zachary Seager 2025
Selection and arrangement copyright © Macmillan Publishers International Ltd. 2025

The Permissions Acknowledgements on p. 191 constitute
an extension of this copyright page.

All rights reserved. No part of this publication may be reproduced,
stored in a retrieval system, or transmitted, in any form or by any means
(electronic, mechanical, photocopying, recording or otherwise)
without the prior written permission of the publisher.

1 3 5 7 9 8 6 4 2

A CIP catalogue record for this book is available from the British Library.

Typeset in Platin by Jouve (UK), Milton Keynes
Printed and bound in China by Imago

This book is sold subject to the condition that it shall not, by way of
trade or otherwise, be lent, hired out, or otherwise circulated without
the publisher's prior consent in any form of binding or cover other than
that in which it is published and without a similar condition including
this condition being imposed on the subsequent purchaser.

Visit **www.panmacmillan.com** to read more
about all our books and to buy them.

Contents

Introduction ix

THE GOOD LIFE

EPICURUS (341 BC–270 BC) 2
Epicurus to Menoeceus
Principal Doctrines

ARISTOTLE (384 BC–322 BC) 21
from *Nichomachean Ethics*

SENECA THE YOUNGER (*c.* 4 BC–*c.* AD 65) 35
On the Happy Life

GEORGE ELIOT (1819–1880) 53
To Sarah Hennell

THE PURSUIT OF HAPPINESS

CHARLES DUDLEY WARNER (1829–1900) 58
The Pursuit of Happiness

JEROME K. JEROME (1859–1927)   68
On Eating and Drinking

ROSE MACAULAY (1881–1958)   83
Reading

ALICE MEYNELL (1847–1922)   96
The Horizon

SAMUEL JOHNSON (1709–1784)   103
On the Proper Means of Regulating Sorrow

HOW TO MAKE THE BEST OF LIFE

SAMUEL BUTLER (1835–1902)   114
How to Make the Best of Life

FANNY FERN (1811–1872)   130
Wishings and Longings

HENRY VAN DYKE (1852–1933)   134
Who Owns the Mountains?

RALPH WALDO EMERSON (1803–1882)   143
Friendship

BERTRAND RUSSELL (1872–1970) 170
Machines and the Emotions

VIRGINIA WOOLF (1882–1941) 184
On the Value of Laughter

Permissions Acknowledgements 191

Introduction

What links philosophers and religious thinkers, novelists and agony aunts, podcasters, wellness brands and the United States Declaration of Independence? One of the oldest problems around, posed as early as Aristotle and much earlier by Confucius, and still in need of a durable answer: the pursuit of happiness – what it is and how to find it.

Is happiness pleasure, contentment, delight or satisfaction, rapture, fulfilment, glee? Is it a mental or spiritual state that comes and goes as it pleases? A goal to be sought? A habit to be cultivated? The opposite of sadness, the absence of pain? Is there a formula for it, an algorithm, an infallible incantation?

Is happiness to be found in 'a good bank account, a good cook, and a good digestion,' as Jean-Jacques Rousseau supposedly claimed?

Is it produced 'not so much by great pieces of good fortune that seldom happen,' in Benjamin Franklin's words, 'as by little advantages that occur every day'? Is it 'the sum of pleasures and pains' and the primary aim of individuals, as Jeremy Bentham suggested? Can we only recognize it once it has passed, as Marcel Proust implied ('every paradise is a paradise lost')? Can it be measured, as so-called happiness economists insist? Is finding happiness the meaning of life? Or is it the other way around – is creating our own meaning the surest and perhaps the only path to happiness? Does something called happiness even exist?

Happiness itself is an enduring question that gives rise to countless others. Once you've defined the slippery concept, tougher tasks await. How do you go about finding it, let alone keeping hold of it?

In the first section of this anthology, some of history's most influential thinkers seek to define happiness. Their broader goal is to understand the foundational ethical question: how should one live?

The Greek philosopher Epicurus lays out his vision for the good life. Often misleadingly known as the philosopher of pleasure, his ideas go well beyond simple slogans about maximizing delight. Aristotle – whose views on human flourishing have had a profound effect on ethical thought from his lifetime (the fourth century BCE) to this day – offers an alternative approach to the same problem. The Roman philosopher Seneca suggests a different route again.

Seneca was a thinker in the Stoic tradition, meaning that his ideas centre on our own virtues. He was especially interested in what we ourselves can or can't control. In the process he makes us responsible for our own happiness – he shows us that in meaningful ways, happiness depends on us and us alone, from the way we approach mundane tasks to how we handle the largest of life's challenges.

George Eliot concludes the first section. Among the most analytical of all novelists and therefore at home with the philosophers, she offers a much-needed note of hope.

The second section pulls the puzzle of happiness from these high philosophical altitudes back down to earth.

Jerome K. Jerome, the comic author best known for *Three Men in a Boat*, encourages us to eat, drink and be merry. The unjustly neglected novelist Rose Macaulay writes about a pleasure not quite as simple as bodily nourishment but that, in the eyes of many, proves every bit as satisfying. Poet and suffragist Alice Meynell points us in dazzling prose towards an enduring source of happiness and hope. Charles Dudley Warner, essayist and author, questions whether we should even look for happiness in the first place. And Samuel Johnson – critic, biographer, playwright, poet and much else besides – offers us advice on dealing with sorrow. He knew something about the question: alongside his titanic efforts to produce in a short space of time what for over a century remained the authoritative dictionary of English, Johnson struggled with what he termed madness or melancholy – historians today describe it as depression.

The final section allies the deep thought of part one with the practical bent of part two. Classic authors such as Virginia Woolf, Bertrand Russell and Ralph Waldo Emerson seek to understand, as the celebrated writer Samuel Butler put it, 'how to make the best of life'. They all touch on paths to happiness that fit with their own passions and personal interests.

The sharply ironic Woolf ponders the value of laughter. Emerson – the sage of Concord and figurehead of a philosophical movement,

Transcendentalism, which insisted on the fundamental goodness of human beings – considers friendship. Still reeling from the First World War, committed pacifist Bertrand Russell reflects on the future of our emotions in a world dominated by machines. And satirically minded Samuel Butler opens his essay as follows: 'I have been asked to speak on the question how to make the best of life, but may as well confess at once that I know nothing about it.'

Is happiness a positive or negative quality, the presence of pleasure or the absence of pain? Is it fulfilment or delight? How can we find it and keep hold of it? The authors in this anthology resolve these questions in different ways. At the same time, however, they all propose an underused but clear path to pleasure and delight, a shortcut to happiness available at any moment – reading their works.

The Good Life

EPICURUS

Epicurus to Menoeceus
Principal Doctrines

Let no one when young delay to study philosophy, nor when he is old grow weary of his study. For no one can come too early or too late to secure the health of his soul. And the man who says that the age for philosophy has either not yet come or has gone by is like the man who says that the age for happiness is not yet come to him, or has passed away. Wherefore both when young and old a man must study philosophy, that as he grows old he may be young in blessings through the grateful recollection of what has been, and that in youth he may be old as well, since he will know no fear of what is to come. We must then meditate on the things that make our happiness, seeing that when that is with us we have all, but when it is absent we do all to win it.

The things which I used unceasingly to commend to you, these do and practice, considering them to be the first principles of the good life. First of all believe that god is a being immortal and blessed, even as the common idea of a god is engraved on men's minds, and do not assign to him anything alien to his immortality or ill-suited to his blessedness: but believe about him everything that can uphold his blessedness and immortality. For gods there are, since the knowledge of them is by clear vision. But they are not such as the many believe them to be: for indeed they do not consistently represent them as they believe them to be. And the impious man is not he who denies the gods of the many, but he who attaches to the gods the beliefs of the many. For the statements of the many about the gods are not conceptions derived from sensation, but false suppositions, according to which the greatest misfortunes befall the wicked and the greatest blessings (the good) by the gift of the gods. For men being accustomed always to their own virtues welcome those like themselves, but regard all that is not of their nature as alien.

Become accustomed to the belief that death is nothing to us. For all good and evil consists in sensation, but death is deprivation of sensation. And therefore a right understanding that death is nothing to us makes the mortality of life enjoyable, not because it adds to it an infinite span of time, but because it takes away the craving for immortality. For there is nothing terrible in life for the man who has truly comprehended that there is nothing terrible in not living. So that the man speaks but idly who says that he fears death not because it will be painful when it comes, but because it is painful in anticipation. For that which gives no trouble when it comes, is but an empty pain in anticipation. So death, the most terrifying of ills, is nothing to us, since so long as we exist, death is not with us; but when death comes, then we do not exist. It does not then concern either the living or the dead, since for the former it is not, and the latter are no more.

But the many at one moment shun death as the greatest of evils, at another (yearn for it) as a respite from the (evils) in life. (But the wise man neither seeks to escape life) nor fears the cessation of life, for neither does life offend him nor does the absence of life seem to be any evil. And just as with food he does not seek simply the larger share and nothing else, but rather the most pleasant, so he seeks to enjoy not the longest period of time, but the most pleasant.

And he who counsels the young man to live well, but the old man to make a good end, is foolish, not merely because of the desirability of life, but also because it is the same training which teaches to live well and to die well. Yet much worse still is the man who says it is good not to be born, but 'once born make haste to pass the gates of Death'. For if he says this from conviction why does he not pass away out of life? For it is open to him to do so, if he had firmly made up his mind to this. But if he speaks in jest, his words are idle among men who cannot receive them.

We must then bear in mind that the future is neither ours, nor yet wholly not ours, so that we may not altogether expect it as sure to come, nor abandon hope of it, as if it will certainly not come.

We must consider that of desires some are natural, others vain, and of the natural some are necessary and others merely natural; and of the necessary some are necessary for happiness, others for the repose of the body, and others for very life. The right understanding of these facts enables us to refer all choice and avoidance to the health of the body and (the soul's) freedom from disturbance, since this is the aim of the life of blessedness. For it is to obtain this end that we always act, namely, to avoid pain and fear. And when this is once secured for us, all the tempest of the soul is dispersed, since the living creature has not to wander as though in search of something that is missing, and to look for some other thing by which he can fulfil the good of the soul and the good of the body. For it is then that we have need of pleasure, when we feel pain owing to the absence of pleasure; (but when we do not feel pain), we no longer need pleasure. And for this cause we call pleasure the beginning and end of the blessed life. For we recognize pleasure as the first good innate in us, and from pleasure we begin every act of choice and avoidance, and to pleasure we return again, using the feeling as the standard by which we judge every good.

And since pleasure is the first good and natural to us, for this very reason we do not choose every pleasure, but sometimes we pass over many pleasures, when greater discomfort accrues to us as the result of them: and similarly we think many pains better than pleasures, since a greater pleasure comes to us when we have endured pains for a long time. Every pleasure then because of its natural kinship to us is good, yet not every pleasure is to be chosen: even as every pain also is an evil, yet not all are always of a nature to be avoided. Yet by a scale of comparison and by the consideration of advantages and disadvantages we must form our judgement on all these matters.

For the good on certain occasions we treat as bad, and conversely the bad as good.

And again independence of desire we think a great good—not that we may at all times enjoy but a few things, but that, if we do not possess many, we may enjoy the few in the genuine persuasion that those have the sweetest pleasure in luxury who least need it, and that all that is natural is easy to be obtained, but that which is superfluous is hard. And so plain savours bring us a pleasure equal to a luxurious diet, when all the pain due to want is removed; and bread and water produce the highest pleasure, when one who needs them puts them to his lips. To grow accustomed therefore to simple and not luxurious diet gives us health to the full, and makes a man alert for the needful employments of life, and when after long intervals we approach luxuries disposes us better towards them, and fits us to be fearless of fortune.

When, therefore, we maintain that pleasure is the end, we do not mean the pleasures of profligates and those that consist in sensuality, as is supposed by some who are either ignorant or disagree with us or do not understand, but freedom from pain in the body and from trouble in the mind. For it is not continuous drinkings and revellings, nor the satisfaction of lusts, nor the enjoyment of fish and other luxuries of the wealthy table, which produce a pleasant life, but sober reasoning, searching out the motives for all choice and avoidance, and banishing mere opinions, to which are due the greatest disturbance of the spirit.

Of all this the beginning and the greatest good is prudence. Wherefore prudence is a more precious thing even than philosophy: for from prudence are sprung all the other virtues, and it teaches us that it is not possible to live pleasantly without living prudently and honourably and justly, (nor, again, to live a life of prudence, honour, and justice) without living pleasantly. For the virtues are by nature bound up with the pleasant life, and the pleasant life is inseparable from them. For indeed who, think you, is a better man than he who holds reverent opinions concerning the gods, and is at all times free from fear of death, and has reasoned out the end ordained by nature? He understands that the limit of good things is easy to fulfill and easy to attain, whereas the course of ills is either short in time or slight in pain: he laughs at (destiny), whom some have introduced as the mistress of all things. (He thinks that with us lies the chief power in determining events, some of which happen by necessity) and some by chance, and some are within our control; for while necessity cannot be called to account, he sees that chance is inconstant, but that which is in our control is subject to no master, and to it are naturally attached praise and blame. For, indeed, it were better to follow the myths about the gods than to become a slave to the destiny of the natural philosophers: for the former suggests a hope of placating the gods by worship, whereas the latter involves a necessity which knows no placation. As to chance, he does not regard it as a god as most men do (for in a god's acts there is no disorder), nor as an uncertain cause (of all things): for he does not believe that good and evil are given by chance to man for the framing of a blessed life, but that opportunities for great good and great evil are afforded by it. He therefore thinks it better to be unfortunate in reasonable action than to prosper in unreason.

For it is better in a man's actions that what is well chosen (should fail, rather than that what is ill chosen) should be successful owing to chance.

Meditate therefore on these things and things akin to them night and day by yourself, and with a companion like to yourself, and never shall you be disturbed waking or asleep, but you shall live like a god among men. For a man who lives among immortal blessings is not like to a mortal being.

Principal Doctrines

I. The blessed and immortal nature knows no trouble itself nor causes trouble to any other, so that it is never constrained by anger or favour. For all such things exist only in the weak.

II. Death is nothing to us: for that which is dissolved is without sensation; and that which lacks sensation is nothing to us.

III. The limit of quantity in pleasures is the removal of all that is painful. Wherever pleasure is present, as long as it is there, there is neither pain of body nor of mind, nor of both at once.

IV. Pain does not last continuously in the flesh, but the acutest pain is there for a very short time, and even that which just exceeds the pleasure in the flesh does not continue for many days at once. But chronic illnesses permit a predominance of pleasure over pain in the flesh.

V. It is not possible to live pleasantly without living prudently and honourably and justly, [nor again to live a life of prudence, honour, and justice] without living pleasantly. And the man who does not possess the pleasant life, is not living prudently and honourably and justly, [and the man who does not possess the virtuous life], cannot possibly live pleasantly.

VI. To secure protection from men anything is a natural good, by which you may be able to attain this end.

VII. Some men wished to become famous and conspicuous, thinking that they would thus win for themselves safety from other men. Wherefore if the life of such men is safe, they have obtained the good which nature craves; but if it is not safe, they do not possess that for which they strove at first by the instinct of nature.

VIII. No pleasure is a bad thing in itself: but the means which produce some pleasures bring with them disturbances many times greater than the pleasures.

IX. If every pleasure could be intensified so that it lasted and influenced the whole organism or the most essential parts of our nature, pleasures would never differ from one another.

X. If the things that produce the pleasures of profligates could dispel the fears of the mind about the phenomena of the sky and death and its pains, and also teach the limits of desires (and of pains), we should never have cause to blame them: for they would be filling themselves full with pleasures from every source and never have pain of body or mind, which is the evil of life.

XI. If we were not troubled by our suspicions of the phenomena of the sky and about death, fearing that it concerns us, and also by our failure to grasp the limits of pains and desires, we should have no need of natural science.

XII. A man cannot dispel his fear about the most important matters if he does not know what is the nature of the universe but suspects the truth of some mythical story. So that without natural science it is not possible to attain our pleasures unalloyed.

XIII. There is no profit in securing protection in relation to men, if things above and things beneath the earth and indeed all in the boundless universe remain matters of suspicion.

XIV. The most unalloyed source of protection from men, which is secured to some extent by a certain force of expulsion, is in fact the immunity which results from a quiet life and the retirement from the world.

XV. The wealth demanded by nature is both limited and easily procured; that demanded by idle imaginings stretches on to infinity.

XVI. In but few things chance hinders a wise man, but the greatest and most important matters reason has ordained and throughout the whole period of life does and will ordain.

XVII. The just man is most free from trouble, the unjust most full of trouble.

XVIII. The pleasure in the flesh is not increased, when once the pain due to want is removed, but is only varied: and the limit as regards pleasure in the mind is begotten by the reasoned understanding of these very pleasures and of the emotions akin to them, which used to cause the greatest fear to the mind.

XIX. Infinite time contains no greater pleasure than limited time, if one measures by reason the limits of pleasure.

XX. The flesh perceives the limits of pleasure as unlimited and unlimited time is required to supply it. But the mind, having attained a reasoned understanding of the ultimate good of the flesh and its limits and having dissipated the fears concerning the time to come, supplies us with the complete life, and we have no further need of infinite time: but neither does the mind shun pleasure, nor, when circumstances begin to bring about the departure from life, does it approach its end as though it fell short in any way of the best life.

XXI. He who has learned the limits of life knows that that which removes the pain due to want and makes the whole of life complete is easy to obtain; so that there is no need of actions which involve competition.

XXII. We must consider both the real purpose and all the evidence of direct perception, to which we always refer the conclusions of opinion; otherwise, all will be full of doubt and confusion.

XXIII. If you fight against all sensations, you will have no standard by which to judge even those of them which you say are false.

XXIV. If you reject any single sensation and fail to distinguish between the conclusion of opinion as to the appearance awaiting confirmation and that which is actually given by the sensation or feeling, or each intuitive apprehension of the mind, you will confound all other sensations as well with the same groundless opinion, so that you will reject every standard of judgement. And if among the mental images created by your opinion you affirm both that which awaits confirmation and that which does not, you will not escape error, since you will have preserved the whole cause of doubt in every judgement between what is right and what is wrong.

XXV. If on each occasion instead of referring your actions to the end of nature, you turn to some other nearer standard when you are making a choice or an avoidance, your actions will not be consistent with your principles.

XXVI. Of desires, all that do not lead to a sense of pain, if they are not satisfied, are not necessary, but involve a craving which is easily dispelled, when the object is hard to procure or they seem likely to produce harm.

XXVII. Of all the things which wisdom acquires to produce the blessedness of the complete life, for the greatest is the possession of friendship.

XXVIII. The same conviction which has given us confidence that there is nothing terrible that lasts for ever or even for long, has also seen the protection of friendship most fully completed in the limited evils of this life.

XXIX. Among desires some are natural (and necessary, some natural) but not necessary, and others neither natural nor necessary, but due to idle imagination.

XXX. Wherever in the case of desires which are physical, but do not lead to a sense of pain, if they are not fulfilled, the effort is intense, such pleasures are due to idle imagination, and it is not owing to their own nature that they fail to be dispelled, but owing to the empty imaginings of the man.

XXXI. The justice which arises from nature is a pledge of mutual advantage to restrain men from harming one another and save them from being harmed.

XXXII. For all living things which have not been able to make compacts not to harm one another or be harmed, nothing ever is either just or unjust; and likewise too for all tribes of men which have been unable or unwilling to make compacts not to harm or be harmed.

XXXIII. Justice never is anything in itself, but in the dealings of men with one another in any place whatever and at any time it is a kind of compact not to harm or be harmed.

XXXIV. Injustice is not an evil in itself, but only in consequence of the fear which attaches to the apprehension of being unable to escape those appointed to punish such actions.

XXXV. It is not possible for one who acts in secret contravention of the terms of the compact not to harm or be harmed, to be confident that he will escape detection, even if at present he escapes a thousand times. For up to the time of death it cannot be certain that he will indeed escape.

XXXVI. In its general aspect justice is the same for all, for it is a kind of mutual advantage in the dealings of men with one another: but with reference to the individual peculiarities of a country or any other circumstances the same thing does not turn out to be just for all.

XXXVII. Among actions which are sanctioned as just by law, that which is proved on examination to be of advantage in the requirements of men's dealings with one another, has the guarantee of justice, whether it is the same for all or not. But if a man makes a law and it does not turn out to lead to advantage in men's dealings with each other, then it no longer has the essential nature of justice. And even if the advantage in the matter of justice shifts from one side to the other, but for a while accords with the general concept, it is none the less just for that period in the eyes of those who do not confound themselves with empty sounds but look to the actual facts.

XXXVIII. Where, provided the circumstances have not been altered, actions which were considered just, have been shown not to accord with the general concept in actual practice, then they are not just. But where, when circumstances have changed, the same actions which were sanctioned as just no longer lead to advantage, there they were just at the time when they were of advantage for the dealings of fellow-citizens with one another; but subsequently they are no longer just, when no longer of advantage.

XXXIX. The man who has best ordered the element of disquiet arising from external circumstances has made those things that he could akin to himself and the rest at least not alien: but with all to which he could not do even this, he has refrained from mixing, and has expelled from his life all which it was of advantage to treat thus.

XL. As many as possess the power to procure complete immunity from their neighbours, these also live most pleasantly with one another, since they have the most certain pledge of security, and after they have enjoyed the fullest intimacy, they do not lament the previous departure of a dead friend, as though he were to be pitied.

ARISTOTLE
from Nichomachean Ethics

Happiness is good activity, not amusement

Now that we have spoken of the virtues, the forms of friendship, and the varieties of pleasure, what remains is to discuss in outline the nature of happiness, since this is what we state the end of human nature to be. Our discussion will be the more concise if we first sum up what we have said already. We said, then, that it is not a disposition; for if it were it might belong to someone who was asleep throughout his life, living the life of a plant, or, again, to someone who was suffering the greatest misfortunes. If these implications are unacceptable, and we must rather class happiness as an activity, as we have said before, and if some activities are necessary, and desirable for the sake of something else, while others are so in themselves, evidently happiness must be placed among those desirable in themselves, not among those desirable for the sake of something else; for happiness does not lack anything, but is self-sufficient. Now those activities are desirable in themselves from which nothing is sought beyond the activity. And of this nature virtuous actions are thought to be; for to do noble and good deeds is a thing desirable for its own sake.

Pleasant amusements also are thought to be of this nature: we choose them not for the sake of other things; for we are injured rather than benefited by them, since we are led to neglect our bodies and our property. But most of the people who are deemed happy take refuge in such pastimes, which is the reason why those who are ready-witted at them are highly esteemed at the courts of tyrants; they make themselves pleasant companions in the tyrants' favourite pursuits, and that is the sort of man they want. Now these things are thought to be of the nature of happiness because people in despotic positions spend their leisure in them, but perhaps such people prove nothing; for virtue and reason, from which good activities flow, do not depend on despotic position; nor, if these people, who have never tasted pure and generous pleasure, take refuge in the bodily pleasures, should these for that reason be thought more desirable; for boys, too, think the things that are valued among themselves are the best. It is to be expected, then, that, as different things seem valuable to boys and to men, so they should to bad men and to good. Now, as we have often maintained, those things are both valuable and pleasant which are such to the good man; and to each man the activity in accordance with his own disposition is most desirable, and therefore to the good man that which is in accordance with virtue. Happiness, therefore, does not lie in amusement; it would, indeed, be strange if the end were amusement, and one were to take trouble and suffer hardship all one's life in order to amuse oneself. For, in a word, everything that we choose we choose for the sake of something else—except happiness, which is an end. Now to exert oneself and work for the sake of amusement seems silly and utterly childish. But to amuse oneself in order that one may exert oneself, as Anacharsis puts it, seems right; for amusement is a sort of relaxation, and we need relaxation because we cannot work continuously. Relaxation, then, is not an end; for it is taken for the sake of activity.

The happy life is thought to be virtuous; now a virtuous life requires exertion, and does not consist in amusement. And we say that serious things are better than laughable things and those connected with amusement, and that the activity of the better of any two things—whether it be two elements of our being or two men—is the more serious; but the activity of the better is *ipso facto* superior and more of the nature of happiness. And any chance person—even a slave—can enjoy the bodily pleasures no less than the best man; but no one assigns to a slave a share in happiness—unless he assigns to him also a share in human life. For happiness does not lie in such occupations, but, as we have said before, in virtuous activities.

Happiness in the highest sense is the contemplative life

If happiness is activity in accordance with virtue, it is reasonable that it should be in accordance with the highest virtue; and this will be that of the best thing in us. Whether it be reason or something else that is this element which is thought to be our natural ruler and guide and to take thought of things noble and divine, whether it be itself also divine or only the most divine element in us, the activity of this in accordance with its proper virtue will be perfect happiness. That this activity is contemplative we have already said.

Now this would seem to be in agreement both with what we said before and with the truth. For, firstly, this activity is the best (since not only is reason the best thing in us, but the objects of reason are the best of knowable objects); and, secondly, it is the most continuous, since we can contemplate truth more continuously than we can *do* anything. And we think happiness ought to have pleasure mingled with it, but the activity of philosophic wisdom is admittedly the pleasantest of virtuous activities; at all events the pursuit of it is thought to offer pleasures marvellous for their purity and their enduringness, and it is to be expected that those who know will pass their time more pleasantly than those who inquire. And the self-sufficiency that is spoken of must belong most to the contemplative activity. For while a philosopher, as well as a just man or one possessing any other virtue, needs the necessaries of life, when they are sufficiently equipped with things of that sort the just man needs people towards whom and with whom he shall act justly, and the temperate man, the brave man, and each of the others is in the same case, but the philosopher, even when by himself, can contemplate truth, and the better the wiser he is; he can perhaps do so better if he has fellow workers, but still he is the most self-sufficient. And this activity alone would seem to be loved for its own sake; for nothing arises from it apart from the contemplating, while from practical activities we gain more or less apart from the action. And happiness is thought to depend on leisure; for we are busy that we may have leisure, and make war that may live in peace. Now the activity of the practical virtues is exhibited in political or military affairs, but the actions concerned with these seem to be unleisurely. Warlike actions are completely so (for no one chooses to be at war, or provokes war, for the sake of being at war; anyone would seem absolutely murderous if he were to make enemies of his friends in order to bring about battle and slaughter); but the action of the statesman also is unleisurely, and aims—beyond the political action itself—at despotic power and honours, or at all events happiness, for him and his fellow citizens—a happiness different from political action, and evidently sought as being different. So if among virtuous actions political and military actions are distinguished by nobility and greatness, and these are unleisurely and aim at an end and are not desirable for their own sake, but the activity of reason, which is contemplative, seems both to be superior in serious worth and to aim at no end beyond itself, and to have its pleasure proper to itself (and this augments the activity), and the self-sufficiency, leisureliness, un-weariedness (so far as this is possible for man), and all the other attributes ascribed to the supremely happy man are evidently those connected with this activity, it follows that this will be the complete happiness of man, if it be allowed a complete term of life (for none of the attributes of happiness is *in*complete).

But such a life would be too high for man; for it is not in so far as he is man that he will live so, but in so far as something divine is present in him; and by so much as this is superior to our composite nature is its activity superior to that which is the exercise of the other kind of virtue. If reason is divine, then, in comparison with man, the life according to it is divine in comparison with human life. But we must not follow those who advise us, being men, to think of human things, and, being mortal, of mortal things, but must, so far as we can, make ourselves immortal, and strain every nerve to live in accordance with the best thing in us; for even if it be small in bulk, much more does it in power and worth surpass everything. This would seem, too, to be each man himself, since it is the authoritative and better part of him. It would be strange, then, if he were to choose not the life of his self but that of something else. And what we said before will apply now: that which is proper to each thing is by nature best and most pleasant for each thing; for man, therefore, the life according to reason is best and pleasantest, since reason more than anything else *is* man. This life therefore is also the happiest.

*Superiority of the contemplative life
further considered*

But in a secondary degree the life in accordance with the other kind of virtue is happy; for the activities in accordance with this befit our human estate. Just and brave acts, and other virtuous acts, we do in relation to each other, observing our respective duties with regard to contracts and services and all manner of actions and with regard to passions; and all of these seem to be typically human. Some of them seem even to arise from the body, and virtue of character to be in many ways bound up with the passions. Practical wisdom, too, is linked to virtue of character, and this to practical wisdom, since the principles of practical wisdom are in accordance with the moral virtues and rightness in morals is in accordance with practical wisdom. Being connected with the passions also, the moral virtues must belong to our composite nature; and the virtues of our composite nature are human; so, therefore, are the life and the happiness which correspond to these. The excellence of the reason is a thing apart: we must be content to say this much about it, for to describe it precisely is a task greater than our purpose requires. It would seem, however, also to need external equipment but little, or less than moral virtue does. Grant that both need the necessaries, and do so equally, even if the statesman's work is the more concerned with the body and things of that sort; for there will be little difference there; but in what they need for the exercise of their activities there will be much difference. The liberal man will need money for the doing of his liberal deeds, and the just man too will need it for the returning of services (for wishes are hard to discern, and even people who are not just pretend to wish to act justly); and the brave man will need power if he is to accomplish any of the acts that correspond to his virtue, and the temperate man will need opportunity; for how else is either he or any of the others to be recognized? It is debated, too, whether the will or the deed is more essential to virtue, which is assumed to involve both; it is surely clear that its perfection involves both; but for deeds many things are needed, and more, the greater and nobler the deeds are. But the man who is contemplating the truth needs no such thing, at least with a view to the exercise of his activity; indeed they are, one may say, even hindrances, at all events to his contemplation; but in so far as he is a man and lives with a number of people, he chooses to do virtuous acts; he will therefore need such aids to living a human life.

But that perfect happiness is a contemplative activity will appear from the following consideration as well. We assume the gods to be above all other beings blessed and happy; but what sort of actions must we assign to them? Acts of justice? Will not the gods seem absurd if they make contracts and return deposits, and so on? Acts of a brave man, then, confronting dangers and running risks because it is noble to do so? Or liberal acts? To whom will they give? It will be strange if they are really to have money or anything of the kind. And what would their temperate acts be? Is not such praise tasteless, since they have no bad appetites? If we were to run through them all, the circumstances of action would be found trivial and unworthy of gods. Still, everyone supposes that they *live* and therefore that they are active; we cannot suppose them to sleep like Endymion. Now if you take away from a living being action, and still more production, what is left but contemplation? Therefore the activity of God, which surpasses all others in blessedness, must be contemplative; and of human activities, therefore, that which is most akin to this must be most of the nature of happiness.

This is indicated, too, by the fact that the other animals have no share in happiness, being completely deprived of such activity. For while the whole life of the gods is blessed, and that of men too in so far as some likeness of such activity belongs to them, none of the other animals is happy, since they in no way share in contemplation. Happiness extends, then, just so far as contemplation does, and those to whom contemplation more fully belongs are more truly happy, not as a mere concomitant but in virtue of the contemplation; for this is in itself precious. Happiness, therefore, must be some form of contemplation.

But, being a man, one will also need external

prosperity; for our nature is not self-sufficient for the purpose of contemplation, but our body also must be healthy and must have food and other attention. Still, we must not think that the man who is to be happy will need many things or great things, merely because he cannot be supremely happy without external goods; for self-sufficiency and action do not involve excess, and we can do noble acts without ruling earth and sea; for even with moderate advantages one can act virtuously (this is manifest enough; for private persons are thought to do worthy acts no less than despots—indeed even more); and it is enough that we should have so much as that; for the life of the man who is active in accordance with virtue will be happy. Solon, too, was perhaps sketching well the happy man when he described him as moderately furnished with externals but as having done (as Solon thought) the noblest acts, and lived temperately; for one can with but moderate possessions do what one ought. Anaxagoras also seems to have supposed the happy man not to be rich nor a despot, when he said that he would not be surprised if the happy man were to seem to most people a strange person; for they judge by externals, since these are all they perceive. The opinions of the wise seem, then, to harmonize with our arguments. But while even such things carry some conviction, the truth in practical matters is discerned from the facts of life; for these are the decisive factor. We must therefore survey what we have already said, bringing it to the test of the facts of life, and if it harmonizes with the facts we must accept it, but if it clashes with them we must suppose it to be mere theory. Now he who exercises his reason and cultivates it seems to be both in the best state of mind and most dear to the gods. For if the gods have any care for human affairs, as they are thought to have, it would be reasonable both that they should delight in that which was best and most akin to them (i.e. reason) and that they should reward those who love and honour this most, as caring for the things that are dear to them and acting both rightly and nobly. And that all these attributes belong most of all to the philosopher is manifest. He, therefore, is the dearest to the gods. And he who is that will presumably be also the happiest; so that in this way too the philosopher will more than any other be happy.

SENECA THE YOUNGER
On the Happy Life

You and I will agree, I think, that outward things are sought for the satisfaction of the body, that the body is cherished out of regard for the soul, and that in the soul there are certain parts which minister to us, enabling us to move and to sustain life, bestowed upon us just for the sake of the primary part of us. In this primary part there is something irrational, and something rational. The former obeys the latter, while the latter is the only thing that is not referred back to another, but rather refers all things to itself. For the divine reason also is set in supreme command over all things, and is itself subject to none; and even this reason which we possess is the same, because it is derived from the divine reason. Now if we are agreed on this point, it is natural that we shall be agreed on the following also—namely, that the happy life depends upon this and this alone:

our attainment of perfect reason. For it is naught but this that keeps the soul from being bowed down, that stands its ground against Fortune; whatever the condition of their affairs may be, it keeps men untroubled. And that alone is a good which is never subject to impairment. That man, I declare, is happy whom nothing makes less strong than he is; he keeps to the heights, leaning upon none but himself; for one who sustains himself by any prop may fall. If the case is otherwise, then things which do not pertain to us will begin to have great influence over us. But who desires Fortune to have the upper hand, or what sensible man prides himself upon that which is not his own?

What is the happy life? It is peace of mind, and lasting tranquility. This will be yours if you possess greatness of soul; it will be yours if you possess the steadfastness that resolutely clings to a good judgment just reached. How does a man reach this condition? By gaining a complete view of truth, by maintaining, in all that he does, order, measure, fitness, and a will that is inoffensive and kindly, that is intent upon reason and never departs therefrom, that commands at the same time love and admiration. In short, to give you the principle in brief compass, the wise man's soul ought to be such as would be proper for a god. What more can one desire who possesses all honourable things? For if dishonourable things can contribute to the best estate, then there will be the possibility of a happy life under conditions which do not include an honourable life. And what is more base or foolish than to connect the good of a rational soul with things irrational? Yet there are certain philosophers who hold that the Supreme Good admits of increase because it is hardly complete when the gifts of fortune are adverse. Even Antipater, one of the great leaders of this school, admits that he ascribes some influence to externals, though only a very slight influence. You see, however, what absurdity lies in not being content with the daylight unless it is increased by a tiny fire. What importance can a spark have in the midst of this clear sunlight? If you are not contented with only that which is honourable, it must follow that you desire in addition either the kind of quiet which the Greeks call "undisturbedness," or else pleasure. But the former may be attained in any case. For the mind is free from disturbance when it is fully free to contemplate the universe, and nothing distracts it from the contemplation of nature. The second, pleasure, is simply the good of cattle.

We are but adding the irrational to the rational, the dishonourable to the honourable. A pleasant physical sensation affects this life of ours; why, therefore, do you hesitate to say that all is well with a man just because all is well with his appetite? And do you rate, I will not say among heroes, but among men, the person whose Supreme Good is a matter of flavours and colours and sounds? Nay, let him withdraw from the ranks of this, the noblest class of living beings, second only to the gods; let him herd with the dumb brutes—an animal whose delight is in fodder!

The irrational part of the soul is twofold: the one part is spirited, ambitious, uncontrolled; its seat is in the passions; the other is lowly, sluggish, and devoted to pleasure. Philosophers have neglected the former, which, though unbridled, is yet better, and is certainly more courageous and more worthy of a man, and have regarded the latter, which is nerveless and ignoble, as indispensable to the happy life. They have ordered reason to serve this latter; they have made the Supreme Good of the noblest living being an abject and mean affair, and a monstrous hybrid, too, composed of various members which harmonize but ill. For as our Vergil, describing Scylla, says:

> Above, a human face and maiden's
>   breast,—
> A beauteous breast,—below, a monster
>   huge
> Of bulk and shapeless, with a dolphin's tail
> Joined to a wolf-like belly.

And yet to this Seylla are tacked on the forms of wild animals, dreadful and swift; but from what monstrous shapes have these wiseacres compounded wisdom! Man's primary art is virtue itself; there is joined to this the useless and fleeting flesh, fitted only for the reception of food, as Posidonius remarks. This divine virtue ends in foulness, and to the higher parts, which are worshipful and heavenly, there is fastened a sluggish and flabby animal. As for the second desideratum,—quiet,—although it would indeed not of itself be of any benefit to the soul, yet it would relieve the soul of hindrances; pleasure, on the contrary, actually destroys the soul and softens all its vigour. What elements so inharmonious as these can be found united? To that which is most vigorous is joined that which is most sluggish, to that which is austere that which is far from serious, to that which is most holy that which is unrestrained even to the point of impurity.

"What, then," comes the retort, "if good health, rest, and freedom from pain are not likely to hinder virtue, shall you not seek all these?" Of course I shall seek them, but not because they are goods,—I shall seek them because they are according to nature and because they will be acquired through the exercise of good judgment on my part. What, then, will be good in them? This alone,—that it is a good thing to choose them. For when I don suitable attire, or walk as I should, or dine as I ought to dine, it is not my dinner, or my walk, or my dress that are goods, but the deliberate choice which I show in regard to them, as I observe, in each thing I do, a mean that conforms with reason. Let me also add that the choice of neat clothing is a fitting object of a man's efforts; for man is by nature a neat and well-groomed animal. Hence the choice of neat attire, and not neat attire in itself, is a good; since the good is not in the thing selected, but in the quality of the selection. Our actions are honourable, but not the actual things which we do. And you may assume that what I have said about dress applies also to the body. For nature has surrounded our soul with the body as with a sort of garment; the body is its cloak. But who has ever reckoned the value of clothes by the wardrobe which contained them? The scabbard does not make the sword good or bad. Therefore, with regard to the body I shall return the same answer to you,—that, if I have the choice, I shall choose health and strength, but that the good involved will be my judgment regarding these things, and not the things themselves.

Another retort is: "Granted that the wise man is happy; nevertheless, he does not attain the Supreme Good which we have defined, unless the means also which nature provides for its attainment are at his call. So, while one who possesses virtue cannot be unhappy, yet one cannot be perfectly happy if one lacks such natural gifts as health, or soundness of limb." But in saying this, you grant the alternative which seems the more difficult to believe,—that the man who is in the midst of unremitting and extreme pain is not wretched, nay, is even happy; and you deny that which is much less serious,—that he is completely happy. And yet, if virtue can keep a man from being wretched, it will be an easier task for it to render him completely happy. For the difference between happiness and complete happiness is less than that between wretchedness and happiness. Can it be possible that a thing which is so powerful as to snatch a man from disaster, and place him among the happy, cannot also accomplish what remains, and render him supremely happy? Does its strength fail at the very top of the climb? There are in life things which are advantageous and disadvantageous,—both beyond our control. If a good man, in spite of being weighed down by all kinds of disadvantages, is not wretched, how is he not supremely happy, no matter if he does lack certain advantages? For as he is not weighted down to wretchedness by his burden of disadvantages, so he is not withdrawn from supreme happiness through lack of any advantages; nay, he is just as supremely happy without the advantages as he is free from wretchedness though under the load of his disadvantages. Otherwise, if his good can be impaired, it can be snatched from him altogether.

A short space above, I remarked that a tiny fire does not add to the sun's light. For by reason of the sun's brightness any light that shines apart from the sunlight is blotted out. "But," one may say, "there are certain objects that stand in the way even of the sunlight." The sun, however, is unimpaired even in the midst of obstacles, and, though an object may intervene and cut off our view thereof, the sun sticks to his work and goes on his course. Whenever he shines forth from amid the clouds, he is no smaller, nor less punctual either, than when he is free from clouds; since it makes a great deal of difference whether there is merely something in the way of his light or something which interferes with his shining. Similarly, obstacles take nothing away from virtue; it is no smaller, but merely shines with less brilliancy. In our eyes, it may perhaps be less visible and less luminous than before; but as regards itself it is the same and, like the sun when he is eclipsed, is still, though in secret, putting forth its strength. Disasters, therefore, and losses, and wrongs, have only the same power over virtue that a cloud has over the sun.

We meet with one person who maintains that a wise man who has met with bodily misfortune is neither wretched nor happy. But he also is in error, for he is putting the results of chance upon a parity with the virtues, and is attributing only the same influence to things that are honourable as to things that are devoid of honour. But what is more detestable and more unworthy than to put contemptible things in the same class with things worthy of reverence! For reverence is due to justice, duty, loyalty, bravery, and prudence; on the contrary, those attributes are worthless with which the most worthless men are often blessed in fuller measure,—such as a sturdy leg, strong shoulders, good teeth, and healthy and solid muscles. Again, if the wise man whose body is a trial to him shall be regarded as neither wretched nor happy, but shall be left in a sort of half-way position, his life also will be neither desirable nor undesirable. But what is so foolish as to say that the wise man's life is not desirable? And what is so far beyond the bounds of credence as the opinion that any life is neither desirable nor undesirable? Again, if bodily ills do not make a man wretched, they consequently allow him to be happy. For things which have no power to change his condition for the worse, have not the power, either, to disturb that condition when it is at its best.

"But," someone will say, "we know what is cold and what is hot; a lukewarm temperature lies between. Similarly, A is happy, and B is wretched, and C is neither happy nor wretched." I wish to examine this figure, which is brought into play against us. If I add to your lukewarm water a larger quantity of cold water, the result will be cold water. But if I pour in a larger quantity of hot water, the water will finally become hot. In the case, however, of your man who is neither wretched nor happy, no matter how much I add to his troubles, he will not be unhappy, according to your argument; hence your figure offers no analogy. Again, suppose that I set before you a man who is neither miserable nor happy. I add blindness to his misfortunes; he is not rendered unhappy. I cripple him; he is not rendered unhappy. I add afflictions which are unceasing and severe; he is not rendered unhappy. Therefore, one whose life is not changed to misery by all these ills is not dragged by them, either, from his life of happiness. Then if, as you say, the wise man cannot fall from happiness to wretchedness, he cannot fall into non-happiness. For how, if one has begun to slip, can one stop at any particular place? That which prevents him from rolling to the bottom, keeps him at the summit. Why, you urge, may not a happy life possibly be destroyed? It cannot even be disjointed; and for that reason virtue is itself of itself sufficient for the happy life.

"But," it is said, "is not the wise man happier if he has lived longer and has been distracted by no pain, than one who has always been compelled to grapple with evil fortune?" Answer me now,—is he any better or more honourable? If he is not, then he is not happier either. In order to live more happily, he must live more rightly; if he cannot do that, then he cannot live more happily either. Virtue cannot be strained tighter, and therefore neither can the happy life, which depends on virtue. For virtue is so great a good that it is not affected by such insignificant assaults upon it as shortness of life, pain, and the various bodily vexations. For pleasure does not deserve that virtue should even glance at it. Now what is the chief thing in virtue? It is the quality of not needing a single day beyond the present, and of not reckoning up the days that are ours; in the slightest possible moment of time virtue completes an eternity of good. These goods seem to us incredible and transcending man's nature; for we measure its grandeur by the standard of our own weakness, and we call our vices by the name of virtue. Furthermore, does it not seem just as incredible that any man in the midst of extreme suffering should say, "I am happy"? And yet this utterance was heard in the very factory of pleasure, when Epicurus said: "To-day and one other day have been the happiest of all!" although in the one case he was tortured by strangury, and in the other by the incurable pain of an ulcerated stomach. Why, then, should those goods which virtue bestows be incredible in the sight of us, who cultivate virtue, when they are found even in those who acknowledge pleasure as their mistress?

These also, ignoble and base-minded as they are, declare that even in the midst of excessive pain and misfortune the wise man will be neither wretched nor happy. And yet this also is incredible,—nay, still more incredible than the other case. For I do not understand how, if virtue falls from her heights, she can help being hurled all the way to the bottom. She either must preserve one in happiness, or, if driven from this position, she will not prevent us from becoming unhappy. If virtue only stands her ground, she cannot be driven from the field; she must either conquer or be conquered.

But some say: "Only to the immortal gods is given virtue and the happy life; we can attain but the shadow, as it were, and semblance of such goods as theirs. We approach them, but we never reach them." Reason, however, is a common attribute of both gods and men; in the gods it is already perfected, in us it is capable of being perfected. But it is our vices that bring us to despair; for the second class of rational being, man, is of an inferior order,—a guardian, as it were, who is too unstable to hold fast to what is best, his judgment still wavering and uncertain. He may require the faculties of sight and hearing, good health, a bodily exterior that is not loathsome, and, besides, greater length of days conjoined with an unimpaired constitution. Though by means of reason he can lead a life which will not bring regrets, yet there resides in this imperfect creature, man, a certain power that makes for badness, because he possesses a mind which is easily moved to perversity. Suppose, however, the badness which is in full view, and has previously been stirred to activity, to be removed; the man is still not a good man, but he is being moulded to goodness. One, however, in whom there is lacking any quality that makes for goodness, is bad.

But

> He in whose body virtue dwells, and spirit
> E'er present,

is equal to the gods; mindful of his origin, he strives to return thither. No man does wrong in attempting to regain the heights from which he once came down. And why should you not believe that something of divinity exists in one who is a part of God? All this universe which encompasses us is one, and it is God; we are associates of God; we are his members. Our soul has capabilities, and is carried thither, if vices do not hold it down. Just as it is the nature of our bodies to stand erect and look upward to the sky, so the soul, which may reach out as far as it will, was framed by nature to this end, that it should desire equality with the gods. And if it makes use of its powers and stretches upward into its proper region it is by no alien path that it struggles toward the heights. It would be a great task to journey heavenwards; the soul but returns thither. When once it has found the road, it boldly marches on, scornful of all things. It casts no backward glance at wealth; gold and silver—things which are fully worthy of the gloom in which they once lay—it values not by the sheen which smites the eyes of the ignorant, but by the mire of ancient days, whence our greed first detached and dug them out.

The soul, I affirm, knows that riches are stored elsewhere than in men's heaped-up treasure-houses; that it is the soul, and not the strong-box, which should be filled. It is the soul that men may set in dominion over all things, and may install as owner of the universe, so that it may limit its riches only by the boundaries of East and West, and, like the gods, may possess all things; and that it may, with its own vast resources, look down from on high upon the wealthy, no one of whom rejoices as much in his own wealth as he resents the wealth of another. When the soul has transported itself to this lofty height, it regards the body also, since it is a burden which must be borne, not as a thing to love, but as a thing to oversee; nor is it subservient to that over which it is set in mastery. For no man is free who is a slave to his body. Indeed, omitting all the other masters which are brought into being by excessive care for the body, the sway which the body itself exercises is captious and fastidious. Forth from this body the soul issues, now with unruffled spirit, now with exultation, and, when once it has gone forth, asks not what shall be the end of the deserted clay. No; just as we do not take thought for the clippings of the hair and the beard, even so that divine soul, when it is about to issue forth from the mortal man, regards the destination of its earthly vessel—whether it be consumed by fire, or shut in by a stone, or buried in the earth, or torn by wild beasts—as being of no more concern to itself than is the afterbirth to a child just born. And whether this body shall be cast out and plucked to pieces by birds, or devoured when

> thrown to the sea-dogs as prey.

how does that concern him who is nothing? Nay, even when it is among the living, the soul fears nothing that may happen to the body after death; for though such things may have been threats, they were not enough to terrify the soul previous to the moment of death. It says: "I am not frightened by the executioner's hook, nor by the revolting mutilation of the corpse which is exposed to the scorn of those who would witness the spectacle. I ask no man to perform the last rites for me; I entrust my remains to none. Nature has made provision that none shall go unburied. Time will lay away one whom cruelty has cast forth." Those were eloquent words which Maecenas uttered:

I want no tomb; for Nature doth provide
For outcast bodies burial.

You would imagine that this was the saying of a man of strict principles. He was indeed a man of noble and robust native gifts, but in prosperity he impaired these gifts by laxness. Farewell.

GEORGE ELIOT
To Sarah Hennell

May, 1844

To begin with business, I send you on the other side the translations you wished (Strauss), but they are perhaps no improvements on what you had done. I shall be very glad to learn from you the particulars as to the mode of publication—who are the parties that will find the funds, and whether the manuscripts are to be put into the hands of any one when complete, or whether they are to go directly from me to the publishers? I was very foolish not to imagine about these things in the first instance, but ways and means are always afterthoughts with me.

You will soon be settled and enjoying the blessed spring and summer time. I hope you are looking forward to it with as much delight as I. One has to spend so many years in learning how to be happy. I am just beginning to make some progress in the science, and I hope to disprove Young's theory that "as soon as we have found the key of life, it opes the gates of death." Every year strips us of at least one vain expectation, and teaches us to reckon some solid good in its stead. I never will believe that our youngest days are our happiest. What a miserable augury for the progress of the race and the destination of the individual, if the more matured and enlightened state is the less happy one! Childhood is only the beautiful and happy time in contemplation and retrospect: to the child it is full of deep sorrows, the meaning of which is unknown. Witness colic and whooping-cough and dread of ghosts, to say nothing of hell and Satan, and an offended Deity in the sky, who was angry when I wanted too much plum-cake. Then the sorrows of older persons, which children see but cannot understand, are worse than all. All this to prove that we are happier than when we were seven years old, and that we shall be happier when we are forty than we are now, which I call a comfortable doctrine, and one worth trying to believe! I am sitting with father, who every now and then jerks off my attention to the history of Queen Elizabeth, which he is reading.

The Pursuit
of Happiness

CHARLES DUDLEY WARNER

The Pursuit of Happiness

Perhaps the most curious and interesting phrase ever put into a public document is "the pursuit of happiness." It is declared to be an inalienable right. It cannot be sold. It cannot be given away. It is doubtful if it could be left by will.

The right of every man to be six feet high, and of every woman to be five feet four, was regarded as self-evident, until women asserted their undoubted right to be six feet high also, when some confusion was introduced into the interpretation of this rhetorical fragment of the eighteenth century.

But the inalienable right to the pursuit of happiness has never been questioned since it was proclaimed as a new gospel for the New World. The American people accepted it with enthusiasm, as if it had been the discovery of a gold-prospector, and started out in the pursuit as if the devil were after them.

If the proclamation had been that happiness is a common right of the race, alienable or otherwise, that all men are or may be happy, history and tradition might have interfered to raise a doubt whether even the new form of government could so change the ethical condition. But the right to make a pursuit of happiness, given in a fundamental bill of rights, had quite a different aspect. Men had been engaged in many pursuits, most of them disastrous, some of them highly commendable. A sect in Galilee had set up the pursuit of righteousness as the only or the highest object of man's immortal powers. The rewards of it, however, were not always immediate. Here was a political sanction of a pursuit that everybody acknowledged to be of a good thing.

Given a heartaching longing in every human being for happiness, here was high warrant for going in pursuit of it. And the curious effect of this *mot d'ordre* was that the pursuit arrested the attention as the most essential, and the happiness was postponed, almost invariably, to some future season, when leisure or plethora, that is, relaxation or gorged desire, should induce that physical and moral glow which is commonly accepted as happiness. This glow of well-being is sometimes called contentment, but contentment was not in the programme. If it came at all, it was only to come after strenuous pursuit, that being the inalienable right.

People, to be sure, have different conceptions of happiness, but whatever they are, it is the custom, almost universal, to postpone the thing itself. This of course is specially true in our American system, where we have a chartered right to the thing itself. Other nations who have no such right may take it out in occasional driblets, odd moments that come, no doubt, to men and races who have no privilege of voting, or to such favoured places as New York city, whose government is always the same, however they vote.

We are all authorised to pursue happiness, and we do as a general thing make a pursuit of it. Instead of simply being happy in the condition where we are, getting the sweets of life in human intercourse, hour by hour, as the bees take honey from every flower that opens in the summer air, finding happiness in the well-filled and orderly mind, in the sane and enlightened spirit, in the self that has become what the self should be, we say that to-morrow, next year, in ten or twenty or thirty years, when we have arrived at certain coveted possessions or situation, we will be happy. Some philosophers dignify this postponement with the name of hope.

Sometimes wandering in a primeval forest, in all the witchery of the woods, besought by the kindliest solicitations of nature, wild flowers in the trail, the call of the squirrel, the flutter of birds, the great world-music of the wind in the pine-tops, the flecks of sunlight on the brown carpet and on the rough bark of immemorial trees, I find myself unconsciously postponing my enjoyment until I shall reach a hoped-for open place of full sun and boundless prospect.

The analogy cannot be pushed, for it is the common experience that these open spots in life, where leisure and space and contentment await us, are usually grown up with thickets, fuller of obstacles, to say nothing of labours and duties and difficulties, than any part of the weary path we have trod.

Why add the pursuit of happiness to our other inalienable worries? Perhaps there is something wrong in ourselves when we hear the complaint so often that men are pursued by disaster instead of being pursued by happiness.

We all believe in happiness as something desirable and attainable, and I take it that this is the underlying desire when we speak of the pursuit of wealth, the pursuit of learning, the pursuit of power in office or in influence, that is, that we shall come into happiness when the objects last named are attained. No amount of failure seems to lessen this belief. It is a matter of experience that wealth and learning and power are as likely to bring unhappiness as happiness, and yet this constant lesson of experience makes not the least impression upon human conduct. I suppose that the reason of this unheeding of experience is that every person born into the world is the only one exactly of that kind that ever was or ever will be created, so that he thinks he may be exempt from the general rules. At any rate, he goes at the pursuit of happiness in exactly the old way, as if it were an original undertaking. Perhaps the most melancholy spectacle offered to us in our short sojourn in this pilgrimage, where the roads are so dusty and the caravansaries so ill provided, is the credulity of this pursuit. Mind, I am not objecting to the pursuit of wealth, or of learning, or of power,—they are all explainable, if not justifiable,—but to the blindness that does not perceive their futility as a means of attaining the end sought, which is happiness, an end that can only be compassed by the right adjustment of each soul to this and to any coming state of existence. For whether the great scholar who is stuffed with knowledge is happier than the great money-getter who is gorged with riches, or the wily politician who is a Warwick in his realm, depends entirely upon what sort of a man this pursuit has made him. There is a kind of fallacy current nowadays that a very rich man, no matter by what unscrupulous means he has gathered an undue proportion of the world into his possession, can be happy if he can turn round and make a generous and lavish distribution of it for worthy purposes. If he has preserved a remnant of conscience, this distribution may give him much satisfaction, and justly increase his good opinion of his own deserts; but the fallacy is in leaving out of account the sort of man he has become in this sort of pursuit. Has he escaped that hardening of the nature, that drying up of the sweet springs of sympathy, which usually attend a long-continued selfish undertaking? Has either he or the great politician or the great scholar cultivated the real sources of enjoyment?

The pursuit of happiness! It is not strange that men call it an illusion. But I am well satisfied that it is not the thing itself, but the pursuit, that is an illusion. Instead of thinking of the pursuit, why not fix our thoughts upon the moments, the hours, perhaps the days, of this divine peace, this merriment of body and mind, that can be repeated and perhaps indefinitely extended by the simplest of all means, namely, a disposition to make the best of whatever comes to us? Perhaps the Latin poet was right in saying that no man can count himself happy while in this life, that is, in a continuous state of happiness; but as there is for the soul no time save the conscious moment called "now," it is quite possible to make that "now" a happy state of existence. The point I make is that we should not habitually postpone that season of happiness to the future.

No one, I trust, wishes to cloud the dreams of youth, or to dispel by excess of light what are called the illusions of hope. But why should the boy be nurtured in the current notion that he is to be really happy only when he has finished school, when he has got a business or profession by which money can be made, when he has come to manhood? The girl also dreams that for her happiness lies ahead, in that springtime when she is crossing the line of womanhood,—all the poets make much of this,—when she is married and learns the supreme lesson how to rule by obeying. It is only when the girl and the boy look back upon the years of adolescence that they realise how happy they might have been then if they had only known they were happy, and did not need to go in pursuit of happiness.

The pitiful part of this inalienable right to the pursuit of happiness is, however, that most men interpret it to mean the pursuit of wealth, and strive for that always, postponing being happy until they get a fortune, and if they are lucky in that, find at the end that the happiness has somehow eluded them, that, in short, they have not cultivated that in themselves that alone can bring happiness. More than that, they have lost the power of the enjoyment of the essential pleasures of life. I think that the woman in the Scriptures who out of her poverty put her mite into the contribution-box got more happiness out of that driblet of generosity and self-sacrifice than some men in our day have experienced in founding a university.

And how fares it with the intellectual man? To be a selfish miser of learning, for self-gratification only, is no nobler in reality than to be a miser of money. And even when the scholar is lavish of his knowledge in helping an ignorant world, he may find that if he has made his studies as a pursuit of happiness he has missed his object. Much knowledge increases the possibility of enjoyment, but also the possibility of sorrow. If intellectual pursuits contribute to an enlightened and altogether admirable character, then indeed has the student found the inner spring of happiness. Otherwise one cannot say that the wise man is happier than the ignorant man.

In fine, and in spite of the political injunction, we need to consider that happiness is an inner condition, not to be raced after. And what an advance in our situation it would be if we could get it into our heads here in this land of inalienable rights that the world would turn round just the same if we stood still and waited for the daily coming of our Lord!

JEROME K. JEROME
On Eating and Drinking

I always was fond of eating and drinking, even as a child—especially eating, in those early days. I had an appetite then, also a digestion. I remember a dull eyed, livid-complexioned gentleman coming to dine at our house once. He watched me eating for about five minutes, quite fascinated, seemingly, and then he turned to my father, with, "Does your boy ever suffer from dyspepsia?"

"I never heard him complain of anything of that kind," replied my father. "Do you ever suffer from dyspepsia, Collywobbles?" (They called me Collywobbles, but it was not my real name.)

"No, pa," I answered. After which, I added, "What is dyspepsia, pa?"

My livid-complexioned friend regarded me with a look of mingled amazement and envy. Then in a tone of infinite pity he slowly said, "You will know—some day."

My poor, dear mother used to say she liked to see me eat, and it has always been a pleasant reflection to me since that I must have given her much gratification in that direction. A growing, healthy lad, taking plenty of exercise, and careful to restrain himself from indulging in too much study, can generally satisfy the most exacting expectations as regards his feeding powers.

It is amusing to see boys eat, when you have not got to pay for it. Their idea of a square meal is a pound and a half of roast beef with five or six good-sized potatoes (soapy ones preferred, as being more substantial), plenty of greens, and four thick slices of Yorkshire pudding, followed by a couple of currant dumplings, a few green apples, and a pen'orth of nuts, half a dozen jumbles, and a bottle of ginger beer. After that they play at horses.

How they must despise us men, who require to sit quiet for a couple of hours after dining off a spoonful of clear soup and the wing of a chicken!

But the boys have not all the advantages on their side. A boy never enjoys the luxury of being satisfied. A boy never feels full. He can never stretch out his legs, put his hands behind his head, and, closing his eyes, sink into the ethereal blissfulness that encompasses the well-dined man. A dinner makes no difference whatever to a boy. To a man, it is as a good fairy's potion, and, after it, the world appears a brighter and a better place. A man who has dined satisfactorily experiences a yearning love toward all his fellow-creatures. He strokes the cat quite gently, and calls it "poor pussy," in tones full of the tenderest emotion. He sympathizes with the members of the German band outside, and wonders if they are cold; and, for the moment, he does not even hate his wife's relations.

A good dinner brings out all the softer side of a man. Under its genial influence, the gloomy and morose become jovial and chatty. Sour, starchy individuals, who all the rest of the day go about looking as if they lived on vinegar and Epsom salts, break out into wreathed smiles after dinner and exhibit a tendency to pat small children on the head, and to talk to them—vaguely—about sixpences. Serious young men thaw, and become mildly cheerful; and snobbish young men, of the heavy mustache type, forget to make themselves objectionable.

I always feel sentimental myself after dinner. It is the only time when I can properly appreciate love stories. Then, when the hero clasps "her" to his heart in one last wild embrace, and stifles a sob, I feel as sad as though I had dealt at whist and turned up only a deuce; and when the heroine dies in the end I weep. If I read the same tale early in the morning, I should sneer at it. Digestion, or rather indigestion, has a marvelous effect upon the heart. If I want to write anything very pathetic—I mean if I want to *try* to write anything very pathetic—I eat a large plateful of hot buttered muffins about an hour beforehand and then, by the time I sit down to my work, a feeling of unutterable melancholy has come over me. I picture heart-broken lovers parting forever at lonely way-side stiles, while the sad twilight deepens around them, and only the tinkling of a distant sheep-bell breaks the sorrowladen silence. Old men sit and gaze at withered flowers till their sight is dimmed by the mist of tears. Little dainty maidens wait and watch at open casements; but "he cometh not," and the heavy years roll by, and the sunny gold tresses wear white and thin. The babies that they dandled have become grown men and women with podgy torments of their own, and the playmates that they laughed with are lying very silent under the waving grass. But still they wait and watch, till the dark shadows of the unknown night steal up and gather round them, and the world with its childish troubles fades from their aching eyes.

I see pale corpses tossed on white-foamed waves, and death-beds stained with bitter tears, and graves in trackless deserts. I hear the wild wailing of women, the low moaning of the little children, the dry sobbing of strong men. It's all the muffins. I could not conjure up one melancholy fancy upon a mutton chop and a glass of champagne.

A full stomach is a great aid to poetry, and indeed no sentiment of any kind can stand upon an empty one. We have not time or inclination to indulge in fanciful troubles, until we have got rid of our real misfortunes. We do not sigh over dead dicky-birds with the bailiff in the house; and, when we do not know where on earth to get our next shilling from, we do not worry whether our mistress's smiles are cold, or hot, or lukewarm, or anything else about them.

Foolish people—when I say "foolish people" in this contemptuous way, I mean people who entertain different opinions to mine. If there is one person I do despise more than another, it is the man who does not think exactly the same on all topics as I do. Foolish people, I say, then, who have never experienced much of either, will tell you that mental distress is far more agonizing than bodily. Romantic and touching theory! so comforting to the love-sick young spring who looks down patronizingly at some poor devil with a white starved face, and thinks to himself, "Ah, how happy you are compared with me!" so soothing to fat old gentlemen who cackle about the superiority of poverty over riches. But it is all nonsense—all cant. An aching head soon makes one forget an aching heart. A broken finger will drive away all recollections of an empty chair. And when a man feels really hungry, he does not feel anything else.

We sleek, well-fed folk can hardly realize what feeling hungry is like. We know what it is to have no appetite, and not to care for the dainty victuals placed before us; but we do not understand what it means to sicken for food—to die for bread while others waste it—to gaze with famished eyes upon coarse fare steaming behind dingy windows, longing for a pen'orth of pease pudding, and not having the penny to buy it—to feel that a crust would be delicious, and that a bone would be a banquet.

Hunger is a luxury to us, a piquant, flavor-giving sauce. It is well worth while to get hungry and thirsty, merely to discover how much gratification can be obtained from eating and drinking. If you wish to thoroughly enjoy your dinner, take a thirty-mile country walk after breakfast, and don't touch anything till you get back. How your eyes will glisten at sight of the white table-cloth and steaming dishes then! With what a sigh of content you will put down the empty beer tankard, and take up your knife and fork! And how comfortable you feel afterward, as you push back your chair, light a cigar, and beam round upon everybody.

Make sure, however, when adopting this plan, that the good dinner is really to be had at the end, or the disappointment is trying. I remember once a friend and I—dear old Joe, it was. Ah! how we lose one another in life's mist. It must be eight years since I last saw Joseph Taboys. How pleasant it would be to meet his jovial face again, to clasp his strong hand, and to hear his cheery laugh once more! He owes me fourteen shillings, too. Well, we were on a holiday together, and one morning we had breakfast early, and started for a tremendously long walk. We had ordered a duck for dinner overnight. We said, "Get a big one, because we shall come home awfully hungry;" and as we were going out our landlady came up in great spirits. She said, "I have got you gentlemen a duck, if you like. If you get through that, you'll do well;" and she held up a bird about the size of a doormat. We chuckled at the sight, and said we would try. We said it with self-conscious pride, like men who know their own power. Then we started.

We lost our way, of course. I always do in the country, and it does make me so wild, because it is no use asking directions of any of the people you meet. One might as well inquire of a lodging-house slavey the way to make beds, as expect a country bumpkin to know the road to the next village. You have to shout the question about three times before the sound of your voice penetrates his skull. At the third time, he slowly raises his head, and stares blankly at you. You yell it at him then for the fourth time, and he repeats it after you. He ponders while you could count a couple of hundred, after which, speaking at the rate of three words a minute, he fancies you "couldn't do better than—" Here he catches sight of another idiot coming down the road, and bawls out to him the particulars, requesting his advice. The two then argue the case for a quarter of an hour or so, and finally agree that you had better go straight down the lane, round to the right, and cross by the third stile, and keep to the left by old Jimmy Milcher's cow-shed and across the seven-acre field, and through the gate by 'Squire Grubbin's hay-stack, keeping the bridle path for a while, till you come opposite the hill where the wind-mill used to be—but it's gone now—and round to the right, leaving Stiggin's plantation behind you; and you say "Thank you," and go away with a splitting headache, but without the faintest notion of your way, the only clear idea you have on the subject being that somewhere or other there is a stile which has to be got over; and at the next turn, you come upon four stiles, all leading in different directions!

We had undergone this ordeal two or three times. We had tramped over fields. We had waded through brooks, and scrambled over hedges and walls. We had had a row as to whose fault it was that we had first lost our way. We had got thoroughly disagreeable, foot-sore, and weary. But, throughout it all, the hope of that duck kept us up. A fairy-like vision, it floated before our tired eyes, and drew us onward.

The thought of it was as a trumpet-call to the fainting. We talked of it, and cheered each other with our recollections of it. "Come along," we said, "the duck will be spoiled."

We felt a strong temptation, at one point, to

turn into a village inn as we passed, and have a cheese and a few loaves between us; but we heroically restrained ourselves: we should enjoy the duck all the better for being famished.

We fancied we smelled it when we got into the town, and did the last quarter of a mile in three minutes. We rushed upstairs and washed ourselves, and changed our clothes, and came down, and pulled our chairs up to the table, and sat and rubbed out hands while the landlady removed the covers, when I seized the knife and fork and started to carve.

It seemed to want a lot of carving. I struggled with it for about five minutes without making the slightest impression, and then Joe, who had been eating potatoes, wanted to know if it wouldn't be better for some one to do the job that understood carving. I took no notice of his foolish remark, but attacked the bird again, and so vigorously this time, that the animal left the dish, and took refuge in the fender.

We soon had it out of that, though, and I was prepared to make another effort. But Joe was getting unpleasant. He said that if he had thought we were to have a game of blind hookey with the dinner, he would have got a bit of bread and cheese outside.

I was too exhausted to argue. I laid down the knife and fork with dignity, and took a side seat; and Joe went for the wretched creature. He worked away, in silence for awhile, and then he muttered: "Damn the duck!" and took his coat off.

We did break the thing up at length, with the aid of a chisel; but it was perfectly impossible to eat it, and we had to make a dinner off the vegetables and an apple tart. We tried a mouthful of the duck, but it was like eating India-rubber.

It was a wicked sin to kill that drake. But there! There's no respect for old institutions in this country.

I started this paper with the idea of writing about eating and drinking, but I seem to have confined my remarks entirely to eating as yet. Well, you see, drinking is one of those subjects with which it is unadvisable to appear too well acquainted. The days are gone by when it was considered manly to go to bed intoxicated every night, and a clear head and a firm hand no longer draw down upon their owner the reproach of effeminacy. On the contrary, in these sadly degenerate days, an evil-smelling breath, a blotchy face, a reeling gait, and a husky voice are regarded as the hall-marks of the cad rather than of the gentleman.

Even nowadays, though, the thirstiness of mankind is something supernatural. We are forever drinking on one excuse or another. A man never feels comfortable unless he has a glass before him. We drink before meals, and with meals, and after meals. We drink when we meet a friend, also when we part from a friend. We drink when we are talking, when we are reading, and when we are thinking. We drink one another's health, and spoil our own. We drink the Queen, and the Army, and the Ladies, and everybody else that is drinkable; and I believe, if the supply ran short, we should drink our mothers-in-law.

By the way, we never eat anybody's health, always drink it. Why should we not stand up now and then and eat a tart to somebody's success?

To me, I confess, the constant necessity of drinking under which the majority of men labor is quite unaccountable. I can understand people drinking to down care, or to drive away maddening thoughts, well enough. I can understand the ignorant masses loving to soak themselves in drink—oh, yes, it's very shocking that they should, of course—very shocking to us who live in cosy homes, with all the graces and pleasures of life around us, that the dwellers in damp cellars and windy attics should creep from their dens of misery into the warmth and glare of the public-house bar, and seek to float for a brief space away from their dull world upon a Lethe stream of gin.

But think, before you hold up your hands in horror at their ill-living, what "life" for these wretched creatures really means. Picture the squalid misery of their brutish existence, dragged on from year to year in the narrow, noisome room where, huddled like vermin in the sewers, they welter, and sicken, and sleep; where dirt-grimed children scream and fight, and sluttish, shrill-voiced women cuff, and curse, and nag; where the street outside teems with roaring filth, and the house around is a bedlam of riot and stench.

Think what a sapless stick this fair flower of life must be to them, devoid of mind and soul. The horse in his stall scents the sweet hay, and munches the ripe corn contentedly. The watchdog in his kennel blinks at the grateful sun, dreams of a glorious chase over the dewy fields, and wakes with a yelp of gladness to greet a caressing hand. But the clod-like life of these human logs never knows one ray of light. From the hour when they crawl from their comfortless bed to the hour when they lounge back into it again, they never live one moment of real life. Recreation, amusement, companionship, they know not the meaning of. Joy, sorrow, laughter, tears, love, friendship, longing, despair, are idle words to them. From the day when their baby eyes first look out upon their sordid world to the day when, with an oath, they close them forever, and their bones are shoveled out of sight, they never warm to one touch of human sympathy, never thrill to a single thought, never start to a single hope. In the name of the God of Mercy let them pour the maddening liquor down their throats, and feel for one brief moment that they live!

Ah! we may talk sentiment as much as we like, but the stomach is the real seat of happiness in this world. The kitchen is the chief temple wherein we worship, its roaring fire is our vestal flame, and the cook is our great high priest. He is a mighty magician and a kindly one. He soothes away all sorrow and care. He drives forth all enmity, gladdens all love. Our God is great, and the cook is his prophet. Let us eat, drink, and be merry.

ROSE MACAULAY
Reading

Here is one of the oddest of the odd inventions which man has sought out, this conveying to one another by marks scratched on paper thoughts privately conceived in the mind. It shows, as all the arts show, the infinite publicism of humankind, the sociability, the interdependence, which cannot endure to have a thought, to conceive a tale, a tune, a picture, an arrangement of words, or anything else, but all must forthwith be informed of it. And how avidly we run to be informed; we have already consumed many thousands of tales, poems, essays, and what not, but we are never satiate, we are greedy always for more. We begin the day by running our eyes over those multi-paged printed rags which furnish us with potted selections of events which have occurred during the last twenty-four hours. What excitement! Here are countries plunging into war, politicians making speeches, governments, aeroplanes and motor-cars crashing right and left, murders, thefts and revolutions, Britons flung into foreign gaols, Etonians bowled by other Etonians in 1887 (they have remembered it ever since, amid all the uproar and confusion of life), outbreaks of healthy-Aryan-national-sentiment in Germany, of sacred egoism in Italy, of foot-and-mouth disease in Berkshire. It has all occurred many times before, it will all occur many times again, but still I devour the pages with eager appetite, stimulated and mildly stunned. My newspaper makes me realise, in the improbable event of my ever forgetting it, on to what an exciting, what a tumultuous world, the sun and I matitutinally rise.

Having risen, I endeavor for a time to bound my reading by what I regard as my proper studies, that is, by the requirements of such labours as I am at the moment committed to. These requirements, generously interpreted, may take me almost anywhere. They may take me, for example, to my dictionary; and, having heaved one of the somewhat ponderous volumes of this mighty work from its shelf (this is one of the main ways in which I keep in good athletic training) I continue to read in it at random, since it would be waste to heave it back at once. I need not expatiate on the inexhaustible pleasure to be extracted from the perusal of this dictionary, from the tasting of this various feast of language, etymology, and elegant extracts from all the periods of English literature. In this enticing pastime a whole morning may fleet itself idly away.

Or, on some slight pretext, the other works that beckon from my shelves like sirens from enchanted seas may win me to them, and, soon oblivious of the reason for my plunge, I am swimming in those deep voluminous seas, among poetry, masques, plays, history, lives, diaries, letters, zoology, navigations and explorations. These, last, above the rest, have the siren's power to drug and to detain. For they are, I suppose, what the psychologists call, in their uncouth tongue, wish-fulfilment, or dream-sublimation. They take you travelling over the globe, and with no further trouble than the lazy flick of a page. Why, as Samuel Purchas introducing his collection of travellers' tales, so plausibly asked, travel, when you can get all the benefits of doing so and suffer none of its damages, by reading of the travels of others? Why should gentlemen adventure themselves to see the fashions of other countries, where their souls and bodies find temptations to a twofold whoredom, and bring home a few smattering terms, flattering garbs, apish cringes, foppish fancies, foolish guises and disguises, the vanities of neighbour nations (I name not Naples) without furthering their knowledge of God, the world or themselves? For his part, for the benefit both of those who cannot travel far and those who cannot travel virtuously, he offers "a world of travellers to their domestic entertainment."

In brief, he recommends to us his travelogue, in which "both elephants may swim in deep voluminous seas, and such as want either lust or leisure may single out what author or voyage shall best fit to his profit or his pleasure." He would have us arm-chair travellers, and well he knew how to play on our indolence.

Here, then, we sit, as he suggests, at home and in peace under the shadow of our own vine and fig, and from the shore behold with safety and delight the dangerous navigations and expeditions of explorers, viewing their war-like fights in the watery plain as from a fortified tower, enjoying the sweet contemplation of their laborious actions. Most commodiously we peregrinate with Marco Polo over Persia, Thibet, Turkistan, and to the court of Khublai Khan; with Spanish Conquistadores and English pirate merchants to Mexico, the Indies, and the New World; with Portugal friars about Abyssinia; with the Hollanders to the Java seas; with King Solomon's navy to Ophir; with Captain William Hawkins, hindered all the way by proud injurious Portugals and wily Jesuits, to the court of the Great Mogul; with Sir John Hawkins in the *Jesus* to take five hundred negroes on the New Guinea coast and make vent of them to Spaniards in the Indies; with the good ship *Dog* to the Mexique Bay; with Captain Knox to the wild Highlands of Ceylon; with Thomas Gage, the disgruntled Jesuit, over Guatemala; with John Chilton over all New Spain, among Indians who dared not eat him for fear he might have the pox; with Anthony Knivet plundering chests of silver from the cells of Portugal friars in Brazil, eating the bark of cinnamon-trees at Port Famine, encountering cannibals, a crocodile, and a great dead whale lying on the shore like a ship grown with moss. We may visit the island of Ferro and see that tree which rains continually; or chase after those flitting isles near Teneriffe which, when men approach them, they vanish; or behold the islands off Scotland swimming after the manner of the ancient Cyclades and flitting up and down in the water, the sport of tempests; on these same islands you may see (and still without moving a step nearer the Scotch express) trees from whose fruit falling into running water ducks and geese do grow. "Whoever took possession of the huge oceans, made procession round about the vast earth? Whoever discovered new constellations, saluted the frozen poles, subjected the burning zones?" Whoever may have done so, I am as good as they, and far more at case, sitting in my armchair and following them about the world with my eyes, doped and lulled with their enchanting lies. Without putting out a hand but to turn a page, I break off a sugar cane and suck it, drop into my mouth pears dripping honey, pluck a store of oysters from the boughs of trees (but these have a flash taste), gather barnacle geese from the barnacle-trees, smell the sweetness of great lemon woods, watch Sierra Leonians slithering up high palm-trees to fill gourds with palmito wine, eat wood fruits called beninganions and beguills, as big as apples and tasting like strawberries, taste cooked friar, but reject it as unwholesome, visit the Castle at Agra, where in a fair court every noon the Rajah sees elephants, lions and buffles fight, and so on to Lahore, the way set on both sides with mulberry-trees; watch a Christian ape at the court of King Jahanjar pick out the name of Christ from those of twelve prophets shuffled in a bag, tearing up the eleven others with distaste; sail up the river Quame for gold, elephants' teeth, ambergris and slaves; find turtles' eggs with Roger Barlow in the Indies, unicorns' horns with Sir John Hawkins in Florida; watch from the Florida beach the sea-fowl chase the flying fish; sail among these huge icy mountains which make such a dashing and crashing one against another in green Arctic seas; voyage, in brief, all oceans, peregrinate all lands, taste all foods, meet all people, enjoy all pleasures.

Meet all people. Yes; my humble dwelling-room becomes a salon, where I receive, without even troubling to rise or bow, an extraordinary miscellaneous crowd or rabble of persons, chattering in all tongues on all topics, in verse, in stately prose, in strolling, colloquial late-Stuart slang, in round and booming Johnsonian, in demure and ladylike Austenian, in sly and delicate Proustian, in gay modern English and French. Many are pompous, foolish, absurd, many have wit, many have ideas, many have neither. Some are wicked above the ordinary, some of a virtue only found among the angels and among earthly citizens of bygone centuries; of these my flat is not worthy, they shine oddly in it. Among them move people "so beastly that they put themself to no manner of labour, but study only how to take their neighbours for to eat them." Theological controversialists too I entertain; I hear the schoolmen thunder against one another on subtle points of doctrine, Jesuits and Jansenists furiously raging together, Puritan and Anglican at it hammer and tongs, non-Jurors smitten by the See of Bangor, the higher mathematics by that of Cloyne. Yet I do not greatly encourage these religious thunderings; I welcome more often blander and gayer guests, finding them apter for a salon. I prefer the urbane smile, the elegant jest, the fit phrase, the lovely line, the strange adventure, the subtle thought, or the sounding period of the historian.

At times, too, I like my salon to become a zoo, a bestiary, a setting for the infinitely strange habits of animals, of unicorns, elephants, dragons, manticoras, remoras, sea-serpents, dolphins, turtles, sparrow-camels, panthers, cockatrices, chameleons, and others of their curious kind.

Another and still more indolent salon I hold in my bed at night, in the hour before sleep. The guests here are of a different kind, less disturbing and exciting, for it does not do to be disturbed and excited before sleep. Poetry will not do at this hour, nor prose of a past and more splendid age.

It is an hour reserved for the narrative fiction or biography of the present moment. As I drift in this agreeable ship towards sleep, I marvel drowsily at its good craftsmanship. How charmingly A writes, I think; how ingenious is B, how C's quick wit makes me smile, how D holds the attention nailed fast, so that if one slips a word one loses a sense. How sharp an irony sparkles from E's pages, how amiable a jester is F, how sound a workman G. How well they, for the most part, write. (Those who do not, do not detain me for more than a few pages.) Surely, I sleepily reflect, the standard of writing has climbed up and up through the past two decades. When I was young, we did not, I am sure, write as well as we nearly all write now. The standard has risen. There are, I believe, floods of tosh; fortunately, unless one is a publisher or a reviewer, one need not see it. But there is enough that interests, pleases or entertains to fill the ante-somnial hour night by night with company good enough for the occasion, which is all that one should demand of current literature.

So much for the home salon. One attends, also, the salons of others. There are within my reach two great places of entertainment. One is in a pleasant square; here one roams at will about gridded galleries, reading what one chooses, removing books by armfuls and leaving them scattered on tables to find their own ways back, or taking them away, either after being entered in ledgers if one is a person of probity, or concealed in dispatch-cases if one is a thief; for this library is a notable hunting-ground for thieves; frail human nature has signally failed under the strain of seeing so many books at once, and the biblioklept, one of the lowest of God's creatures, may be prowling next you along those quiet corridors, his stealthy hand plucking the desired fruit from the bough and stowing it furtively away.

This is less possible in the other great London resort of readers, where they know better than to trust us. Here we are fed liberally, afforded every kindness, but we are marked men and women, we cannot easily steal away with pockets full of volumes. Unless, indeed, we chanced to be newcomers, gave false names, and were careful not to return. Something in this sort might, I suppose, be managed. But for most of us the strait and narrow way of rectitude is indicated.

We can, however, lick our fingers to turn the pages. I have been told that some readers even lick the pages direct with the tongue, but this habit is, I believe, confined to those who have been allowed special access to books not generally accessible, and denotes some peculiar pleasure.

For my part, I find it enough to sit drowsily in a great circular room, my wants supplied (in God's good time) by attendant elves, a great bank climbing volume by volume about me, shutting me off from the inky little student writing a research thesis on my right, and from the patriarch from the far deserts of Arabia on my left, leaving me dreamily alone, transcribing from crabbed texts in a crabbed hand, languishing agreeably in that hot-house clime, all the books in the world (or as near as makes no matter to me) within the call of a written order.

What is the extraordinary pleasure that we derive from this pastime? Why do we forget everything for it, feel by it transported, enlarged, enslaved, freed, impassioned, enlivened, soothed, drugged, delighted, distressed, entertained, sharpened in wits, ennobled in soul, winged in imagination, gratified in humour, stirred to pity, rage, love, rapture, enthusiasm, creation, zeal for learning, infinite zest and curiosity for life? I do not know, nor anyone.

And, in the end, it wears down our eyes, never intended for this strange and crabbed use, so that we have to read through discs of magnifying glass. As to our health—"the man whom about midnight, when others take their rest, thou seest come out of his study meagre-looking . . . squalid, and spauling, dost thou think that plodding on his books he doth seek how he shall become an honester man . . . ? There is no such matter."

No, indeed. Still, he has enjoyed his reading.

ALICE MEYNELL

The Horizon

To mount a hill is to lift with you something lighter and brighter than yourself or than any meaner burden. You lift the world, you raise the horizon; you give a signal for the distance to stand up. It is like the scene in the Vatican when a Cardinal, with his dramatic Italian hands, bids the kneeling groups to arise. He does more than bid them. He lifts them, he gathers them up, far and near, with the upward gesture of both arms; he takes them to their feet with the compulsion of his expressive force. Or it is as when a conductor takes his players to successive heights of music. You summon the sea, you bring the mountains, the distances unfold unlooked-for wings and take an even flight. You are but a man lifting his weight upon the upward road, but as you climb the circle of the world goes up to face you.

Not here or there, but with a definite continuity, the unseen unfolds. This distant hill outsoars that less distant, but all are on the wing, and the plain raises its verge. All things follow and wait upon your eyes. You lift these up, not by the raising of your eyelids, but by the pilgrimage of your body. "Lift thine eyes to the mountains." It is then that other mountains lift themselves to your human eyes.

It is the law whereby the eye and the horizon answer one another that makes the way up a hill so full of universal movement. All the landscape is on pilgrimage. The town gathers itself closer, and its inner harbours literally come to light; the headlands repeat themselves; little cups within the treeless hills open and show their farms. In the sea are many regions. A breeze is at play for a mile or two, and the surface is turned. There are roads and curves in the blue and in the white. Not a step of your journey up the height that has not its replies in the steady motion of land and sea. Things rise together like a flock of many-feathered birds.

But it is the horizon, more than all else, you have come in search of; that is your chief companion on your way. It is to uplift the horizon to the equality of your sight that you go high. You give it a distance worthy of the skies. There is no distance, except the distance in the sky, to be seen from the level earth; but from the height is to be seen the distance of this world. The line is sent back into the remoteness of light, the verge is removed beyond verge, into a distance that is enormous and minute.

So delicate and so slender is the distant horizon that nothing less near than Queen Mab and her chariot can equal its fineness. Here on the edges of the eyelids, or there on the edges of the world—we know no other place for things so exquisitely made, so thin, so small and tender. The touches of her passing, as close as dreams, or the utmost vanishing of the forest or the ocean in the white light between the earth and the air; nothing else is quite so intimate and fine. The extremities of a mountain view have just such tiny touches as the closeness of closing eyes shut in.

On the horizon is the sweetest light. Elsewhere colour mars the simplicity of light; but there colour is effaced, not as men efface it, by a blur or darkness; but by mere light. The bluest sky disappears on that shining edge; there is not substance enough for colour. The rim of the hill, of the woodland, of the meadowland, of the sea—let it only be far enough—has the same absorption of colour; and even the dark things drawn upon the bright edges of the sky are lucid, the light is among them, and they are mingled with it. The horizon has its own way of making bright the penciled figures of forests, which are black but luminous.

On the horizon, moreover, closes the long perspective of the sky. There you perceive that an ordinary sky of clouds—not a thunder sky—is not a wall but the underside of a floor. You see the clouds that repeat each other grow smaller by distance; and you find a new unity in the sky and earth that gather alike the great lines of their designs to the same distant close. There is no longer an alien sky, tossed up in unintelligible heights.

Of all the things that London has forgone, the most to be regretted is the horizon. Not the bark of the trees in its right colour; not the spirit of the growing grass, which has in some way escaped from the parks; not the smell of the earth unmingled with the odour of soot; but rather the mere horizon. No doubt the sun makes a beautiful thing of the London smoke at times, and in some places of the sky; but not there, not where the soft sharp distance ought to shine. To be dull there is to put all relations and comparisons in the wrong, and to make the sky lawless.

A horizon dark with storm is another thing. The weather darkens the line and defines it, or mingles it with the raining cloud; or softly dims it, or blackens it against a gleam of narrow sunshine in the sky. The stormy horizon will take wing, and the sunny. Go high enough, and you can raise the light from beyond the shower, and the shadow from behind the ray. Only the shapeless and lifeless smoke disobeys and defeats the summons of the eyes.

Up at the top of the seaward hill your first thought is one of some compassion for sailors, inasmuch as they see but little of their sea. A child on a mere Channel cliff looks upon spaces and sizes that they cannot see in the Pacific, on the ocean side of the world. Never in the solitude of the blue water, never between the Cape of Good Hope and Cape Horn, never between the Islands and the West, has the seaman seen anything but a little circle of sea. The Ancient Mariner, when he was alone, did but drift through a thousand narrow solitudes. The sailor has nothing but his mast, indeed. And but for his mast he would be isolated in as small a world as that of a traveller through the plains.

A close circlet of waves is the sailor's famous offing. His offing hardly deserves the name of horizon. To hear him you might think something of his offing, but you do not so when you sit down in the centre of it.

As the upspringing of all things at your going up the heights, so steady, so swift, is the subsidence at your descent. The further sea lies away, hill folds down behind hill. The whole upstanding world, with its looks serene and alert, its distant replies, its signals of many miles, its signs and communications of light, gathers down and pauses. This flock of birds which is the mobile landscape wheels and goes to earth. The Cardinal weighs down the audience with his downward hands. Farewell to the most delicate horizon.

SAMUEL JOHNSON

On the Proper Means of Regulating Sorrow

Tuesday, August 28, 1750

Of the passions which the mind of man is agitated, it may be observed, that they naturally hasten towards their own extinction, by inciting and quickening the attainment of their objects. Thus fear urges our flight, and desire animates our progress; and if there are some which perhaps may be indulged till they outgrow the good appropriated to their satisfaction, as it is frequently observed of avarice and ambition, yet their immediate tendency is to some means of happiness really existing, and generally within the prospect. The miser always imagines that there is a certain sum that will fill his heart to the brim, and every ambitious man, like king Pyrrhus, has an acquisition in his thoughts that is to terminate his labours, after which he shall pass the rest of his life in ease or gaiety, in repose or devotion.

Sorrow is perhaps the only affection of the breast that can be excepted from this general remark, and it therefore deserves the particular attention of those who have assumed the arduous province of preserving the balance of the mental constitution. The other passions are diseases indeed, but they necessarily direct us to their proper cure. A man at once feels the pain and knows the medicine, to which he is carried with greater haste as the evil which requires it is more excruciating, and cures himself by unerring instinct, as the wounded stags of Crete are related by Ælian to have recourse to vulnerary herbs. But for sorrow there is no remedy provided by nature; it is often occasioned by accidents irreparable, and dwells upon objects that have lost or changed their existence; it requires what it cannot hope, that the laws of the universe should be repealed; that the dead should return, or the past should be recalled.

Sorrow is not that regret for negligence or error which may animate us to a future care or activity, or that repentance of crimes for which, however irrevocable, our Creator has promised to accept it as an atonement; the pain which arises from these causes has very salutary effects, and is every hour extenuating itself by the reparation of those miscarriages that produce it. Sorrow is properly that state of the mind in which our desires are fixed upon the past, without looking forward to the future, an incessant wish that something were otherwise than it has been, a tormenting and harassing want of some enjoyment or possession which we have lost, and which no endeavours can possibly regain. Into such anguish many have sunk upon some sudden diminution of their fortune, an unexpected blast of their reputation, or the loss of children or of friends. They have suffered all sensibility of pleasure to be destroyed by a single blow, have given up for ever the hopes of substituting any other object in the room of that which they lament, resigned their lives to gloom and despondency, and worn themselves out in unavailing misery.

Yet so much is this passion the natural consequence of tenderness and endearment, that, however painful and however useless, it is justly reproachful not to feel it on some occasions; and so widely and constantly has it always prevailed, that the laws of some nations, and the customs of others, have limited a time for the external appearances of grief caused by the dissolution of close alliances, and the breach of domestic union.

It seems determined by the general suffrage of mankind, that sorrow is to a certain point laudable, as the offspring of love, or at least pardonable, as the effect of weakness; but that it ought not to be suffered to increase by indulgence, but must give way, after a stated time, to social duties, and the common avocations of life. It is at first unavoidable, and therefore must be allowed, whether with or without our choice; it may afterwards be admitted as a decent and affectionate testimony of kindness and esteem; something will be extorted by nature, and something may be given to the world. But all beyond the bursts of passion, or the forms of solemnity, is not only useless, but culpable; for we have no right to sacrifice, to the vain longings of affection, that time which Providence allows us for the task of our station.

Yet it too often happens that sorrow, thus lawfully entering, gains such a firm possession of the mind, that it is not afterwards to be ejected; the mournful ideas, first violently impressed and afterwards willingly received, so much engross the attention, as to predominate in every thought, to darken gaiety, and perplex ratiocination. An habitual sadness seizes upon the soul, and the faculties are chained to a single object, which can never be contemplated but with hopeless uneasiness.

From this state of dejection it is very difficult to rise to cheerfulness and alacrity; and therefore many who have laid down rules of intellectual health, think preservatives easier than remedies, and teach us not to trust ourselves with favourite enjoyments, not to indulge the luxury of fondness, but to keep our minds always suspended in such indifference, that we may change the objects about us without emotion.

An exact compliance with this rule might, perhaps, contribute to tranquillity, but surely it would never produce happiness. He that regards none so much as to be afraid of losing them, must live for ever without the gentle pleasures of sympathy and confidence; he must feel no melting fondness, no warmth of benevolence, nor any of those honest joys which nature annexes to the power of pleasing. And as no man can justly claim more tenderness than he pays, he must forfeit his share in that officious and watchful kindness which love only can dictate, and those lenient endearments by which love only can soften life. He may justly be overlooked and neglected by such as have more warmth in their heart; for who would be the friend of him, whom, with whatever assiduity he may be courted, and with services obliged, his principles will not suffer to make equal returns, and who, when you have exhausted all the instances of good-will, can only be prevailed on not to be an enemy?

An attempt to preserve life in a state of neutrality and indifference, is unreasonable and vain. If by excluding joy we could shut out grief, the scheme would deserve very serious attention; but since, however we may debar ourselves from happiness, misery will find its way at many inlets, and the assaults of pain will force our regard, though we may withhold it from the invitations of pleasure, we may surely endeavour to raise life above the middle point of apathy at one time, since it will necessarily sink below it at another.

But though it cannot be reasonable not to gain happiness for fear of losing it, yet it must be confessed, that in proportion to the pleasure of possession, will be for some time our sorrow for the loss; it is therefore the province of the moralist to inquire whether such pains may not quickly give way to mitigation. Some have thought that the most certain way to clear the heart from its embarrassment is to drag it by force into scenes of merriment. Others imagine, that such a transition is too violent, and recommend rather to soothe it into tranquillity, by making it acquainted with miseries more dreadful and afflictive, and diverting to the calamities of others the regards which we are inclined to fix too closely upon our own misfortunes.

It may be doubted whether either of those remedies will be sufficiently powerful. The efficacy of mirth it is not always easy to try, and the indulgence of melancholy may be suspected to be one of those medicines, which will destroy, if it happens not to cure.

The safe and general antidote against sorrow is employment. It is commonly observed, that among soldiers and seamen, though there is much kindness, there is little grief; they see their friend fall without any of that lamentation which is indulged in security and idleness, because they have no leisure to spare from the care of themselves; and whoever shall keep his thoughts equally busy, will find himself equally unaffected with irretrievable losses.

Time is observed generally to wear out sorrow, and its effects might doubtless be accelerated by quickening the succession, and enlarging the variety of objects.

> ———*Si tempore longo*
> *Leniri poterit luctus, tu sperne morari;*
> *Qui sapiet, sibi tempus erit.*—GROTIUS.
> 'Tis long ere time can mitigate your grief;
> To wisdom fly, she quickly brings relief.
> —F. LEWIS.

Sorrow is a kind of rust of the soul, which every new idea contributes in its passage to scour away. It is the putrefaction of stagnant life, and is remedied by exercise and motion.

How to Make the Best of Life

SAMUEL BUTLER

How to Make the Best of Life

I have been asked to speak on the question how to make the best of life, but may as well confess at once that I know nothing about it. I cannot think that I have made the best of my own life, nor is it likely that I shall make much better of what may or may not remain to me. I do not even know how to make the best of the twenty minutes that your committee has placed at my disposal, and as for life as a whole, who ever yet made the best of such a colossal opportunity by conscious effort and deliberation? In little things no doubt deliberate and conscious effort will help us, but we are speaking of large issues, and such kingdoms of heaven as the making the best of these come not by observation.

The question, therefore, on which I have undertaken to address you is, as you must all know, fatuous, if it be faced seriously. Life is like playing a violin solo in public and learning the instrument as one goes on. One cannot make the best of such impossibilities, and the question is doubly fatuous until we are told which of our two lives—the conscious or the unconscious—is held by the asker to be the truer life. Which does the question contemplate—the life we know, or the life which others may know, but which we know not?

Death gives a life to some men and women compared with which their so-called existence here is as nothing. Which is the truer life of Shakespeare, Handel, that divine woman who wrote the "Odyssey," and of Jane Austen—the life which palpitated with sensible warm motion within their own bodies, or that in virtue of which they are still palpitating in ours? In whose consciousness does their truest life consist—their own, or ours? Can Shakespeare be said to have begun his true life till a hundred years or so after he was dead and buried? His physical life was but as an embryonic stage, a coming up out of darkness, a twilight and dawn before the sunrise of that life of the world to come which he was to enjoy hereafter. We all live for a while after we are gone hence, but we are for the most part stillborn, or at any rate die in infancy, as regards that life which every age and country has recognised as higher and truer than the one of which we are now sentient. As the life of the race is larger, longer, and in all respects more to be considered than that of the individual, so is the life we live in others larger and more important than the one we live in ourselves. This appears nowhere perhaps more plainly than in the case of great teachers, who often in the lives of their pupils produce an effect that reaches far beyond anything produced while their single lives were yet unsupplemented by those other lives into which they infused their own.

Death to such people is the ending of a short life, but it does not touch the life they are already living in those whom they have taught; and happily, as none can know when he shall die, so none can make sure that he too shall not live long beyond the grave; for the life after death is like money before it—no one can be sure that it may not fall to him or her even at the eleventh hour. Money and immortality come in such odd unaccountable ways that no one is cut off from hope. We may not have made either of them for ourselves, but yet another may give them to us in virtue of his or her love, which shall illumine us for ever, and establish us in some heavenly mansion whereof we neither dreamed nor shall ever dream. Look at the Doge Loredano Loredani, the old man's smile upon whose face has been reproduced so faithfully in so many lands that it can never henceforth be forgotten—would he have had one hundredth part of the life he now lives had he not been linked awhile with one of those heavensent men who know *che cosa è amor*? Look at Rembrandt's old woman in our National Gallery; had she died before she was eighty-three years old she would not have been living now. Then, when she was eighty-three, immortality perched upon her as a bird on a withered bough.

I seem to hear some one say that this is a mockery, a piece of special pleading, a giving of stones to those that ask for bread. Life is not life unless we can feel it, and a life limited to a knowledge of such fraction of our work as may happen to survive us is no true life in other people; salve it as we may, death is not life any more than black is white.

The objection is not so true as it sounds. I do not deny that we had rather not die, nor do I pretend that much even in the case of the most favoured few can survive them beyond the grave. It is only because this is so that our own life is possible; others have made room for us, and we should make room for others in our turn without undue repining. What I maintain is that a not inconsiderable number of people do actually attain to a life beyond the grave which we can all feel forcibly enough, whether they can do so or not—that this life tends with increasing civilisation to become more and more potent, and that it is better worth considering, in spite of its being unfelt by ourselves, than any which we have felt or can ever feel in our own persons.

Take an extreme case. A group of people are photographed by Edison's new process—say Titiens, Trebelli, and Jenny Lind, with any two of the finest men singers the age has known—let them be photographed incessantly for half an hour while they perform a scene in "Lohengrin"; let all be done stereoscopically. Let them be photographed at the same time so that their minutest shades of intonation are preserved, let the slides be coloured by a competent artist, and then let the scene be called suddenly into sight and sound, say a hundred years hence. Are those people dead or alive? Dead to themselves they are, but while they live so powerfully and so livingly in us, which is the greater paradox—to say that they are alive or that they are dead? To myself it seems that their life in others would be more truly life than their death to themselves is death. Granted that they do not present all the phenomena of life—who ever does so even when he is held to be alive? We are held to be alive because we present a sufficient number of living phenomena to let the others go without saying; those who see us take the part for the whole here as in everything else, and surely, in the case supposed above, the phenomena of life predominate so powerfully over those of death, that the people themselves must be held to be more alive than dead. Our living personality is, as the word implies, only our mask, and those who still own such a mask as I have supposed have a living personality. Granted again that the case just put is an extreme one; still many a man and many a woman has so stamped him or herself on his work that, though we would gladly have the aid of such accessories as we doubtless presently shall have to the livingness of our great dead, we can see them very sufficiently through the master pieces they have left us.

As for their own unconsciousness I do not deny it. The life of the embryo was unconscious before birth, and so is the life—I am speaking only of the life revealed to us by natural religion—after death. But as the embryonic and infant life of which we were unconscious was the most potent factor in our after life of consciousness, so the effect which we may unconsciously produce in others after death, and it may be even before it on those who have never seen us, is in all sober seriousness our truer and more abiding life, and the one which those who would make the best of their sojourn here will take most into their consideration.

Unconsciousness is no bar to livingness. Our conscious actions are a drop in the sea as compared with our unconscious ones. Could we know all the life that is in us by way of circulation, nutrition, breathing, waste and repair, we should learn what an infinitesimally small part consciousness plays in our present existence; yet our unconscious life is as truly life as our conscious life, and though it is unconscious to itself it emerges into an indirect and vicarious consciousness in our other and conscious self, which exists but in virtue of our unconscious self. So we have also a vicarious consciousness in others. The unconscious life of those that have gone before us has in great part moulded us into such men and women as we are, and our own unconscious lives will in like manner have a vicarious consciousness in others, though we be dead enough to it in ourselves.

If it is again urged that it matters not to us how much we may be alive in others, if we are to know nothing about it, I reply that the common instinct of all who are worth considering gives the lie to such cynicism. I see here present some who have achieved, and others who no doubt will achieve, success in literature. Will one of them hesitate to admit that it is a lively pleasure to her to feel that on the other side of the world some one may be smiling happily over her work, and that she is thus living in that person though she knows nothing about it? Here it seems to me that true faith comes in. Faith does not consist, as the Sunday School pupil said, "in the power of believing that which we know to be untrue." It consists in holding fast that which the healthiest and most kindly instincts of the best and most sensible men and women are intuitively possessed of, without caring to require much evidence further than the fact that such people are so convinced; and for my own part I find the best men and women I know unanimous in feeling that life in others, even though we know nothing about it, is nevertheless a thing to be desired and gratefully accepted if we can get it either before death or after. I observe also that a large number of men and women do actually attain to such life, and in some cases continue so to live, if not for ever, yet to what is practically much the same thing. Our life then in this world is, to natural religion as much as to revealed, a period of probation. The use we make of it is to settle how far we are to enter into another, and whether that other is to be a heaven of just affection or a hell of righteous condemnation.

Who, then, are the most likely so to run that they may obtain this veritable prize of our high calling? Setting aside such lucky numbers drawn as it were in the lottery of immortality, which I have referred to casually above, and setting aside also the chances and changes from which even immortality is not exempt, who on the whole are most likely to live anew in the affectionate thoughts of those who never so much as saw them in the flesh, and know not even their names? There is a *nisus*, a straining in the dull dumb economy of things, in virtue of which some, whether they will it and know it or no, are more likely to live after death than others, and who are these? Those who aimed at it as by some great thing that they would do to make them famous? Those who have lived most in themselves and for themselves, or those who have been most ensouled consciously, but perhaps better unconsciously, directly but more often indirectly, by the most living souls past and present that have flitted near them? Can we think of a man or woman who grips us firmly, at the thought of whom we kindle when we are alone in our honest daw's plumes, with none to admire or shrug his shoulders, can we think of one such, the secret of whose power does not lie in the charm of his or her personality—that is to say, in the wideness of his or her sympathy with, and therefore life in and communion with other people? In the wreckage that comes ashore from the sea of time there is much tinsel stuff that we must preserve and study if we would know our own times and people; granted that many a dead charlatan lives long and enters largely and necessarily into our own lives; we use them and throw them away when we have done with them. I do not speak of these, I do not speak of the Virgils and Alexander Popes, and who can say how many more whose names I dare not mention for fear of offending. They are as stuffed birds or beasts in a Museum; serviceable no doubt from a scientific standpoint, but with no vivid or vivifying hold upon us. They seem to be alive, but are not. I am speaking of those who do actually live in us, and move us to higher achievements though they be long dead, whose life thrusts out our own and overrides it. I speak of those who draw us ever more towards them from youth to age, and to think of whom is to feel at once that we are in the hands of those we love, and whom we would most wish to resemble. What is the secret of the hold that these people have upon us? Is it not that while, conventionally speaking, alive, they most merged their lives in, and were in fullest communion with those among whom they lived? They found their lives in losing them. We never love the memory of any one unless we feel that he or she was himself or herself a lover.

I have seen it urged, again, in querulous accents, that the so-called immortality even of the most immortal is not for ever. I see a passage to this effect in a book that is making a stir as I write. I will quote it. The writer says:—

"So, it seems to me, is the immortality we so glibly predicate of departed artists. If they survive at all, it is but a shadowy life they live, moving on through the gradations of slow decay to distant but inevitable death. They can no longer, as heretofore, speak directly to the hearts of their fellow-men, evoking their tears or laughter, and all the pleasures, be they sad or merry, of which imagination holds the secret. Driven from the marketplace they become first the companions of the student, then the victims of the specialist. He who would still hold familiar intercourse with them must train himself to penetrate the veil which in ever-thickening folds conceals them from the ordinary gaze; he must catch the tone of a vanished society, he must move in a circle of alien associations, he must think in a language not his own."

This is crying for the moon, or rather pretending to cry for it, for the writer is obviously insincere. I see the *Saturday Review* says the passage I have just quoted "reaches almost to poetry," and indeed I find many blank verses in it, some of them very aggressive. No prose is free from an occasional blank verse, and a good writer will not go hunting over his work to rout them out, but nine or ten in little more than as many lines is indeed reaching too near to poetry for good prose. This, however, is a trifle, and might pass if the tone of the writer was not so obviously that of cheap pessimism. I know not which is cheapest, pessimism or optimism. One forces lights, the other darks; both are equally untrue to good art, and equally sure of their effect with the groundlings. The one extenuates, the other sets down in malice. The first is the more amiable lie, but both are lies, and are known to be so by those who utter them. Talk about catching the tone of a vanished society to understand Rembrandt or Giovanni Bellini! It is nonsense—the folds do not thicken in front of these men; we understand them as well as those among whom they went about in the flesh, and perhaps better. Homer and Shakespeare speak to us probably far more effectually than they did to the men of their own time, and most likely we have them at their best. I cannot think that Shakespeare talked better than we hear him now in "Hamlet" or "Henry the Fourth"; like enough he would have been found a very disappointing person in a drawing-room. People stamp themselves on their work; if they have not done so they are naught, if they have we have them; and for the most part they stamp themselves deeper on their work than on their talk. No doubt Shakespeare and Handel will be one day clean forgotten, as though they had never been born. The world will in the end die; mortality therefore itself is not immortal, and when death dies the life of these men will die with it—but not sooner. It is enough that they should live within us and move us for many ages as they have and will. Such immortality, therefore, as some men and women are born to, achieve, or have thrust upon them, is a practical if not a technical immortality, and he who would have more let him have nothing.

I see I have drifted into speaking rather of how to make the best of death than of life, but who can speak of life without his thoughts turning instantly to that which is beyond it? He or she who has made the best of the life after death has made the best of the life before it; who cares one straw for any such chances and changes as will commonly befall him here if he is upheld by the full and certain hope of everlasting life in the affections of those that shall come after? If the life after death is happy in the hearts of others, it matters little how unhappy was the life before it.

And now I leave my subject, not without misgiving that I shall have disappointed you. But for the great attention which is being paid to the work from which I have quoted above, I should not have thought it well to insist on points with which you are, I doubt not, as fully impressed as I am: but that book weakens the sanctions of natural religion, and minimises the comfort which it affords us, while it does more to undermine than to support the foundations of what is commonly called belief. Therefore I was glad to embrace this opportunity of protesting. Otherwise I should not have been so serious on a matter that transcends all seriousness. Lord Beaconsfield cut it shorter with more effect. When asked to give a rule of life for the son of a friend he said, "Do not let him try and find out who wrote the letters of Junius." Pressed for further counsel he added, "Nor yet who was the man in the iron mask"— and he would say no more. Don't bore people. And yet I am by no means sure that a good many people do not think themselves ill-used unless he who addresses them has thoroughly well bored them—especially if they have paid any money for hearing him. My great namesake said, "Surely the pleasure is as great of being cheated as to cheat," and great as the pleasure both of cheating and boring undoubtedly is, I believe he was right. So I remember a poem which came out some thirty years ago in *Punch*, about a young lady who went forth in quest to "Some burden make or burden bear, but which she did not greatly care, oh Miserie." So, again, all the holy men and women who in the Middle Ages professed to have discovered how to make the best of life took care that being bored, if not cheated, should have a large place in their programme. Still there are limits, and I close not without fear that I may have exceeded them.

FANNY FERN
Wishings and Longings

Did you never *wish* you had it? Of course you have, a thousand times. You never would be miserable any more if it could only be so. You are sure of that. It may be a fine house, a fine store, a fine carriage. No matter what; the desire for it has taken the spice and flavor out of every blessing you possess. I used to play with a little girl once, who told me in confidence, and in pantalettes, "that she should never be happy till she had a real *true* gold watch; and that she meant to be married, as soon as ever she could, to a rich man who would give her one." For myself, I had much rather at that time have had a bunch of flowers, and I didn't suppose she really meant what she said, as she stood there tying on her doll's bonnet. But she was in dead earnest, though I *didn't* know it. Sure enough, she got her rich husband, and her gold watch; and was sick enough of both, as I have since found out, before the honeymoon was well over.

One day I heard a boy say to his younger brother, who was crying lustily, "Now, Tom, I know you don't want anything, but what do you *think* you want?" That boy was a philosopher, and went to the root of the matter. It is not what we really want, but what we *think* we want, that frets most of us. Perhaps you tell me that you suffer just as much as if your longing were a reasonable or a sensible one. That's true too; but if you only could snatch *to-day's* legitimate happiness, instead of wondering if you could not get a great deal more, for that to-morrow which may never come to you, wouldn't it be wiser? The other day I went off into the woods, with a dear little girl, who is much more of a poetess than a philosopher. Not a patch of soft green moss, not the tiniest bud of a wild flower, or flitting butterfly, or bird, or tree-shadow on the smooth clear lake, escaped her bright, glad eyes. The *first* flower she found enraptured her, and she climbed quite a steep rock with her mites of feet for the second, and so on till her tiny hands were full. Just then she found quite a bunch of bright pink blossoms; and I was so glad for her; when suddenly she burst into such a grieved, piteous cry, "Oh dear! oh dear! what *shall* I do? *I can't hold them all.*"

If we'd only think of that! That "we can't hold them all." That in order to grasp that which is the moment's wish, we must let something else drop that we prize. Something that we can never retrace our steps, in life's devious paths, to reclaim. It may be health, or character, or life itself, for that which is so perishable, so unsatisfying, so harmful, that we can never cease wondering how the "glamour" of it could have so dazzled our mental and moral vision. The little child I speak of, who clambered up the rock to secure that *one* flower, was happier in its possession than with the myriads that she afterwards found lying at her very feet. She had *earned* that one! She had encountered a fierce briar-bush; she had got her hands scratched in the conflict; she had tickled her little nose with a defiant twig; she had tangled her curls; she had scraped her little fat knee till it was red—and *got it!* All herself, too! I couldn't elaborate a better moral, if I preached an hour. We don't value happiness in heaps. It is the one little sweet blossom, that comes unexpectedly in our way, that we love best after all. Isn't it so?

HENRY VAN DYKE

Who Owns the Mountains?

"My heart is fixed firm and stable in the belief that ultimately the sunshine and the summer, the flowers and the azure sky, shall become, as it were, interwoven into man's existence. He shall take from all their beauty and enjoy their glory."
—Richard Jefferies: *The Life of the Fields.*

It was the little lad that asked the question; and the answer also, as you will see, was mainly his.

We had been keeping Sunday afternoon together in our favourite fashion, following out that pleasant text which tells us to "behold the fowls of the air." There is no injunction of Holy Writ less burdensome in acceptance, or more profitable in obedience, than this easy out-of-doors commandment. For several hours we walked in the way of this precept, through the untangled woods that lie behind the Forest

Hills Lodge, where a pair of pigeon-hawks had their nest; and around the brambly shores of the small pond, where Maryland yellow-throats and song-sparrows were settled; and under the lofty hemlocks of the fragment of forest across the road, where rare warblers flitted silently among the tree-tops. The light beneath the evergreens was growing dim as we came out from their shadow into the widespread glow of the sunset, on the edge of a grassy hill, overlooking the long valley of the Gale River, and uplooking to the Franconia Mountains.

It was the benediction hour. The placid air of the day shed a new tranquility over the consoling landscape. The heart of the earth seemed to taste a repose more perfect than that of common days. A hermit-thrush, far up the vale, sang his vesper hymn; while the swallows, seeking their evening meal, circled above the riverfields without an effort, twittering softly, now and then, as if they must give thanks. Slight and indefinable touches in the scene, perhaps the mere absence of the tiny human figures passing along the road or laboring in the distant meadows, perhaps the blue curls of smoke rising lazily from the farmhouse chimneys, or the family groups sitting under the maple-trees before the door, diffused a Sabbath atmosphere over the world.

Then said the lad, lying on the grass beside me, "Father, who owns the mountains?"

I happened to have heard, the day before, of two or three lumber companies that had bought some of the woodland slopes; so I told him their names, adding that there were probably a good many different owners, whose claims taken all together would cover the whole Franconia range of hills.

"Well," answered the lad, after a moment of silence, "I don't see what difference that makes. Everybody can look at them."

They lay stretched out before us in the level sunlight, the sharp peaks outlined against the sky, the vast ridges of forest sinking smoothly towards the valleys, the deep hollows gathering purple shadows in their bosoms, and the little foothills standing out in rounded promontories of brighter green from the darker mass behind them.

Far to the east, the long comb of Twin Mountain extended itself back into the untrodden wilderness. Mount Garfield lifted a clear-cut pyramid through the translucent air. The huge bulk of Lafayette ascended majestically in front of us, crowned with a rosy diadem of rocks. Eagle

Cliff and Bald Mountain stretched their line of scalloped peaks across the entrance to the Notch. Beyond that shadowy vale, the swelling summits of Cannon Mountain rolled away to meet the tumbling waves of Kinsman, dominated by one loftier crested billow that seemed almost ready to curl and break out of green silence into snowy foam. Far down the sleeping Landaff valley the undulating dome of Moosilauke trembled in the distant blue.

They were all ours, from crested cliff to wooded base. The solemn groves of firs and spruces, the plumed sierras of lofty pines, the stately pillared forests of birch and beech, the wild ravines, the tremulous thickets of silvery poplar, the bare peaks with their wide outlooks, and the cool vales resounding with the ceaseless song of little rivers,—we knew and loved them all; they ministered peace and joy to us; they were all ours, though we held no title-deeds and our ownership had never been recorded.

What is property, after all? The law says there are two kinds, real and personal. But it seems to me that the only real property is that which is truly personal, that which we take into our inner life and make our own forever, by understanding and admiration and sympathy and love.

This is the only kind of possession that is worth anything.

A gallery of great paintings adorns the house of the Honourable Midas Bond, and every year adds a new treasure to his collection. He knows how much they cost him, and he keeps the run of the quotations at the auction sales, congratulating himself as the price of the works of his well-chosen artists rises in the scale, and the value of his art treasures is enhanced. But why should he call them his? He is only their custodian. He keeps them well varnished, and framed in gilt. But he never passes through those gilded frames into the world of beauty that lies behind the painted canvas. He knows nothing of those lovely places from which the artist's soul and hand have drawn their inspiration. They are closed and barred to him. He has bought the pictures, but he cannot buy the key. The poor art student who wanders through his gallery, lingering with awe and love before the masterpieces, owns them far more truly than Midas does.

Pomposus Silverman purchased a rich library a few years ago. The books were rare and costly. That was the reason why Pomposus bought them. He was proud to feel that he was the possessor of literary treasures which were not to be found in the houses of his wealthiest acquaintances. But the threadbare Bücherfreund, who was engaged at a slender salary to catalogue the library and take care of it, became the real proprietor. Pomposus paid for the books, but Bücherfreund enjoyed them.

I do not mean to say that the possession of much money is always a barrier to real wealth of mind and heart. Nor would I maintain that all the poor of this world are rich in faith and heirs of the kingdom. But some of them are. And if some of the rich of this world (through the grace of Him with whom all things are possible) are also modest in their tastes, and gentle in their hearts, and open in their minds, and ready to be pleased with unbought pleasures, they simply share in the best things which are provided for all.

I speak not now of the strife that men wage over the definition and the laws of property. Doubtless there is much here that needs to be set right. There are men and women in the world who are shut out from the right to earn a living, so poor that they must perish for want of daily bread, so full of misery that there is no room for the tiniest seed of joy in their lives. This is the lingering shame of civilisation. Some day, perhaps, we shall find the way to banish it. Some day, every man shall have his title to a share in the world's great work and the world's large joy.

But meantime it is certain that, where there are a hundred poor bodies who suffer from physical privation, there are a thousand poor souls who suffer from spiritual poverty. To relieve this greater suffering there needs no change of laws, only a change of heart.

What does it profit a man to be the landed proprietor of countless acres unless he can reap the harvest of delight that blooms from every rood of God's earth for the seeing eye and the loving spirit? And who can reap that harvest so closely that there shall not be abundant gleaning left for all mankind? The most that a wide estate can yield to its legal owner is a living. But the real owner can gather from a field of goldenrod, shining in the August sunlight, an unearned increment of delight.

We measure success by accumulation. The measure is false. The true measure is appreciation. He who loves most has most.

How foolishly we train ourselves for the work of life! We give our most arduous and eager efforts to the cultivation of those faculties which will serve us in the competitions of the forum and the market-place. But if we were wise, we should care infinitely more for the unfolding of those inward, secret, spiritual powers by which alone we can become the owners of anything that is worth having. Surely God is the great proprietor. Yet all His works He has given away. He holds no title-deeds. The one thing that is His, is the perfect understanding, the perfect joy, the perfect love, of all things that He has made. To a share in this high ownership He welcomes all who are poor in spirit. This is the earth which the meek inherit. This is the patrimony of the saints in light.

"Come, laddie," I said to my comrade, "let us go home. You and I are very rich. We own the mountains. But we can never sell them, and we don't want to."

RALPH WALDO EMERSON

Friendship

We have a great deal more kindness than is ever spoken. Maugre all the selfishness that chills like east winds the world, the whole human family is bathed with an element of love like a fine ether. How many persons we meet in houses, whom we scarcely speak to, whom yet we honour, and who honour us! How many we see in the street, or sit with in church, whom, though silently, we warmly rejoice to be with! Read the language of these wandering eye-beams. The heart knoweth.

The effect of the indulgence of this human affection is a certain cordial exhilaration. In poetry, and in common speech, the emotions of benevolence and complacency which are felt towards others are likened to the material effects of fire; so swift, or much more swift, more active, more cheering, are these fine inward irradiations. From the highest degree of passionate love, to the lowest degree of good-will, they make the sweetness of life.

Our intellectual and active powers increase with our affection. The scholar sits down to write, and all his years of meditation do not furnish him with one good thought or happy expression; but it is necessary to write a letter to a friend,—and, forthwith, troops of gentle thoughts invest themselves, on every hand, with chosen words. See, in any house where virtue and self-respect abide, the palpitation which the approach of a stranger causes. A commended stranger is expected and announced, and an uneasiness betwixt pleasure and pain invades all the hearts of a household. His arrival almost brings fear to the good hearts that would welcome him. The house is dusted, all things fly into their places, the old coat is exchanged for the new, and they must get up a dinner if they can. Of a commended stranger, only the good report is told by others, only the good and new is heard by us. He stands to us for humanity. He is what we wish. Having imagined and invested him, we ask how we should stand related in conversation and action with such a man, and are uneasy with fear. The same idea exalts conversation with him. We talk better than we are wont. We have the nimblest fancy, a richer memory, and our dumb devil has taken leave for the time. For long hours we can continue a series of sincere, graceful, rich communications, drawn from the oldest, secretest experience, so that they who sit by, of our own kinsfolk and acquaintance, shall feel a lively surprise at our unusual powers. But as soon as the stranger begins to intrude his partialities, his definitions, his defects, into the conversation, it is all over. He has heard the first, the last, and best he will ever hear from us. He is no stranger now. Vulgarity, ignorance, misapprehension are old acquaintances. Now, when he comes, he may get the order, the dress, and the dinner,—but the throbbing of the heart, and the communications of the soul, no more.

What is so pleasant as these jets of affection which make a young world for me again? What so delicious as a just and firm encounter of two, in a thought, in a feeling? How beautiful, on their approach to this beating heart, the steps and forms of the gifted and the true! The moment we indulge our affections, the earth is metamorphosed; there is no winter, and no night; all tragedies, all ennuis, vanish,—all duties even; nothing fills the proceeding eternity but the forms all radiant of beloved persons. Let the soul be assured that somewhere in the universe it should rejoin its friend, and it would be content and cheerful alone for a thousand years.

I awoke this morning with devout thanksgiving for my friends, the old and the new. Shall I not call God the Beautiful, who daily showeth himself so to me in his gifts? I chide society, I embrace solitude, and yet I am not so ungrateful as not to see the wise, the lovely, and the noble-minded, as from time to time they pass my gate. Who hears me, who understands me, becomes mine,—a possession for all time. Nor is nature so poor but she gives me this joy several times, and thus we weave social threads of our own, a new web of relations; and, as many thoughts in succession substantiate themselves, we shall by-and-by stand in a new world of our own creation, and no longer strangers and pilgrims in a traditionary globe. My friends have come to me unsought. The great God gave them to me. By oldest right, by the divine affinity of virtue with itself. I find them, or rather not I, but the Deity in me and in them derides and cancels the thick walls of individual character, relation, age, sex, circumstance, at which he usually connives, and now makes many one. High thanks I owe you, excellent lovers, who carry out the world for me to new and noble depths, and enlarge the meaning of all my thoughts. These are new poetry of the first Bard,—poetry without stop,—hymn, ode, and epic, poetry still flowing, Apollo and the Muses chanting still. Will these, too, separate themselves from me again, or some of them? I know not, but I fear it not; for my relation to them is so pure, that we hold by simple affinity, and, the Genius of my life being thus social, the same affinity will exert its energy on whomsoever is as noble as these men and women, wherever I may be.

I confess to an extreme tenderness of nature on this point. It is almost dangerous to me to 'crush the sweet poison of misused wine' of the affections. A new person is to me a great event, and hinders me from sleep. I have often had fine fancies about persons which have given me delicious hours; but the joy ends in the day; it yields no fruit. Thought is not born of it; my action is very little modified. I must feel pride in my friend's accomplishments as if they were mine, and a property in his virtues. I feel as warmly when he is praised, as the lover when he hears applause of his engaged maiden. We over-estimate the conscience of our friend. His goodness seems better than our goodness, his nature finer, his temptations less. Everything that is his,—his name, his form, his dress, books, and instruments,—fancy enhances. Our own thought sounds new and larger from his mouth.

Yet the systole and diastole of the heart are not without their analogy in the ebb and flow of love. Friendship, like the immortality of the soul, is too good to be believed. The lover, beholding his maiden, half knows that she is not verily that which he worships; and in the golden hour of friendship, we are surprised with shades of suspicion and unbelief. We doubt that we bestow on our hero the virtues in which he shines, and afterwards worship the form to which we have ascribed this divine inhabitation. In strictness, the soul does not respect men as it respects itself. In strict science all persons underlie the same condition of an infinite remoteness. Shall we fear to cool our love by mining for the metaphysical foundation of this Elysian temple? Shall I not be as real as the things I see? If I am, I shall not fear to know them for what they are. Their essence is not less beautiful than their appearance, though it needs finer organs for its apprehension. The root of the plant is not unsightly to science, though for chaplets and festoons we cut the stem short. And I must hazard the production of the bald fact amidst these pleasing reveries, though it should prove an Egyptian skull at our banquet.

A man who stands united with his thought conceives magnificently of himself. He is conscious of a universal success, even though bought by uniform particular failures. No advantages, no powers, no gold or force, can be any match for him. I cannot choose but rely on my own poverty more than on your wealth. I cannot make your consciousness tantamount to mine. Only the star dazzles; the planet has a faint, moon-like ray. I hear what you say of the admirable parts and tried temper of the party you praise, but I see well that for all his purple cloaks I shall not like him, unless he is at last a poor Greek like me. I cannot deny it, O friend, that the vast shadow of the Phenomenal includes thee also in its pied and painted immensity,—thee also, compared with whom all else is shadow. Thou art not my soul, but a picture and effigy of that. Thou hast come to me lately, and already thou art seizing thy hat and cloak. Is it not that the soul puts forth friends as the tree puts forth leaves, and presently, by the germination of new buds, extrudes the old leaf? The law of nature is alternation for evermore. Each electrical state superinduces the opposite. The soul environs itself with friends, that it may enter into a grander self-acquaintance or solitude; and it goes alone for a season, that it may exalt its conversation or society. This method betrays itself along the whole history of our personal relations. The instinct of affection revives the hope of union with our mates, and the returning sense of insulation recalls us from the chase. Thus every man passes his life in the search after friendship, and if he should record his true sentiment, he might write a letter like this to each new candidate for his love:—

> 'DEAR FRIEND,—If I was sure of thee, sure of thy capacity, sure to match my mood with thine, I should never think again of trifles in relation to thy comings and goings. I am not very wise; my moods are quite attainable, and I respect thy genius; it is to me as yet unfathomed; yet dare I not presume in thee a perfect intelligence of me, and so thou art to me a delicious torment. Thine ever, or never.'

Yet these uneasy pleasures and fine pains are for curiosity, and not for life. They are not to be indulged. This is to weave cobweb, and not cloth. Our friendships hurry to short and poor conclusions, because we have made them a texture of wine and dreams, instead of the tough fibre of the human heart. The laws of friendship are austere and eternal, of one web with the laws of nature and of morals. But we have aimed at a swift and petty benefit, to suck a sudden sweetness. We snatch at the slowest fruit in the whole garden of God, which many summers and many winters must ripen. We seek our friend not sacredly, but with an adulterate passion which would appropriate him to ourselves. In vain. We are armed all over with subtle antagonisms, which, as soon as we meet, begin to play, and translate all poetry into stale prose. Almost all people descend to meet. All association must be a compromise, and, what is worst, the very flower and aroma of the flower of each of the beautiful natures disappears as they approach each other. What a perpetual disappointment is actual society, even of the virtuous and gifted! After interviews have been compassed with long foresight, we must be tormented presently by baffled blows, by sudden, unseasonable apathies, by epilepsies of wit and of animal spirits, in the heyday of friendship and thought. Our faculties do not play us true, and both parties are relieved by solitude.

I ought to be equal to every relation. It makes no difference how many friends I have, and what content I can find in conversing with each, if there be one to whom I am not equal. If I have shrunk unequal from one contest, the joy I find in all the rest becomes mean and cowardly. I should hate myself, if then I made my other friends my asylum:—

> 'The valiant warrior famoused for fight,
> After a hundred victories, once foiled,
> Is from the book of honour razed quite
> And all the rest forgot for which he toiled.'

Our impatience is thus sharply rebuked. Bashfulness and apathy are a tough husk, in which a delicate organisation is protected from premature ripening. It would be lost if it knew itself before any of the best souls were yet ripe enough to know and own it. Respect the 'naturlangsamkeit' which hardens the ruby in a million years, and works in duration, in which Alps and Andes come and go as rainbows. The good spirit of our life has no heaven which is the price of rashness. Love, which is the essence of God, is not for levity, but for the total worth of man. Let us not have this childish luxury in our regards, but the austerest worth; let us approach our friend with an audacious trust in the truth of his heart, in the breadth, impossible to be overturned, of his foundations.

The attractions of this subject are not to be resisted, and I leave, for the time, all account of subordinate social benefit, to speak of that select and sacred relation which is a kind of absolute, and which even leaves the language of love suspicious and common, so much is this purer, and nothing is so much divine.

I do not wish to treat friendships daintily, but with roughest courage. When they are real, they are not glass threads or frostwork, but the solidest thing we know. For now, after so many ages of experience, what do we know of nature, or of ourselves? Not one step has man taken toward the solution of the problem of his destiny. In one condemnation of folly stand the whole universe of men. But the sweet sincerity of joy and peace, which I draw from this alliance with my brother's soul, is the nut itself whereof all nature and all thought is but the husk and shell. Happy is the house that shelters a friend! It might well be built, like a festal bower or arch, to entertain him a single day. Happier, if he know the solemnity of that relation, and honour its law! He who offers himself a candidate for that covenant comes up, like an Olympian, to the great games, where the first-born of the world are the competitors. He proposes himself for contests where Time, Want,

Danger, are in the lists, and he alone is victor who has truth enough in his constitution to preserve the delicacy of his beauty from the wear and tear of all these. The gifts of fortune may be present or absent, but all the speed in that contest depends on intrinsic nobleness, and the contempt of trifles. There are two elements that go to the composition of friendship, each so sovereign that I can detect no superiority in either, no reason why either should be first named. One is Truth. A friend is a person with whom I may be sincere. Before him I may think aloud. I am arrived at last in the presence of a man so real and equal, that I may drop even those undermost garments of dissimulation, courtesy, and second thought, which men never put off, and may deal with him with the simplicity and wholeness with which one chemical atom meets another. Sincerity is the luxury allowed, like diadems and authority, only to the highest rank, that being permitted to speak truth, as having none above it to court or conform unto. Every man alone is sincere. At the entrance of a second person, hypocrisy begins. We parry and fend the approach of our fellow-man by compliments, by gossip, by amusements, by affairs. We cover up our thought from him under a hundred folds. I knew a man who, under a certain religious frenzy, cast off this drapery, and omitting all compliment and commonplace, spoke to the conscience of every person he encountered, and that with great insight and beauty. At first he was resisted, and all men agreed he was mad. But persisting, as indeed he could not help doing, for some time in this course, he attained to the advantage of bringing every man of his acquaintance into true relations with him. No man would think of speaking falsely with him, or of putting him off with any chat of markets or reading-rooms. But every man was constrained by so much sincerity to the like plain dealing, and what love of nature, what poetry, what symbol of truth he had, he did certainly show him. But to most of us society shows not its face and eye, but its side and its back. To stand in true relations with men in a false age is worth a fit of insanity, is it not? We can seldom go erect. Almost every man we meet requires some civility,—requires to be humoured; he has some fame, some talent, some whim of religion or philanthropy in his head that is not to be questioned, and which spoils all conversation with him. But a friend is a sane man who exercises not my ingenuity, but me. My friend gives me entertainment without requiring any stipulation on my part. A friend, therefore, is a sort of paradox in nature. I who alone am, I who see nothing in nature whose existence I can affirm with equal evidence to my own, behold now the semblance of my being, in all its height, variety, and curiosity, reiterated in a foreign form; so that a friend may well be reckoned the masterpiece of nature.

The other element of friendship is tenderness. We are holden to men by every sort of tie, by blood, by pride, by fear, by hope, by lucre, by lust, by hate, by admiration, by every circumstance and badge and trifle, but we can scarce believe that so much character can subsist in another as to draw us by love. Can another be so blessed, and we so pure, that we can offer him tenderness? When a man becomes dear to me, I have touched the goal of fortune. I find very little written directly to the heart of this matter in books. And yet I have one text which I cannot choose but remember. My author says: 'I offer myself faintly and bluntly to those whose I effectually am, and tender myself least to him to whom I am the most devoted.' I wish that friendship should have feet, as well as eyes and eloquence. It must plant itself on the ground before it vaults over the moon. I wish it to be a little of a citizen before it is quite a cherub. We chide the citizen because he makes love a commodity. It is an exchange of gifts, of useful loans; it is good neighbourhood; it watches with the sick; it holds the pall at the funeral; and quite loses sight of the delicacies and nobility of the relation. But though we cannot find the god under this disguise of a sutler, yet, on the other hand, we cannot forgive the poet if he spins his thread too fine, and does not substantiate his romance by the municipal virtues of justice, punctuality, fidelity, and pity. I hate the prostitution of the name of friendship to signify modish and worldly alliances. I much prefer the company of ploughboys and tinpedlars, to the silken and perfumed amity which celebrates its days of encounter by a frivolous display, by rides in a curricle, and dinners at the best taverns. The end of friendship is a commerce the most strict and homely that can be joined; more strict than any of which we have experience. It is for aid and comfort through all the relations and passages of life and death. It is fit for serene days, and graceful gifts, and country rambles, but also for rough roads and hard fare, shipwreck, poverty, and persecution. It keeps company with the sallies of the wit and the trances of religion. We are to dignify to each other the daily needs and offices of man's life, and embellish it by courage, wisdom, and unity. It should never fall into something usual and settled, but should be alert and inventive, and add rhyme and reason to what was drudgery.

Friendship may be said to require natures so rare and costly, each so well tempered and so happily adapted, and withal so circumstanced (for even in that particular, a poet says, love demands that the parties be altogether paired), that its satisfaction can very seldom be assured. It cannot subsist in its perfection, say some of those who are learned in this warm lore of the heart, betwixt more than two. I am not quite so strict in my terms, perhaps because I have never known so high a fellowship as others. I please my imagination more with a circle of godlike men and women variously related to each other, and between whom subsists a lofty intelligence. But I find this law of one to one peremptory for conversation, which is the practice and consummation of friendship. Do not mix waters too much. The best mix as ill as good and bad. You shall have very useful and cheering discourse at several times with two several men, but let all three of you come together, and you shall not have one new and hearty word. Two may talk and one may hear, but three cannot take part in a conversation of the most sincere and searching sort. In good company there is never such discourse between two, across the table, as takes place when you leave them alone. In good company, the individuals merge their egotism into a social soul exactly co-extensive with the several consciousnesses there present. No partialities of friend to friend, no fondnesses of brother to sister, of wife to husband, are there pertinent, but quite otherwise. Only he may then speak who can sail on the common thought of the party, and not poorly limited to his own. Now this convention, which good sense demands, destroys the high freedom of great conversation, which requires an absolute running of two souls into one.

No two men but, being left alone with each other, enter into simpler relations. Yet it is affinity that determines which two shall converse. Unrelated men give little joy to each other, will never suspect the latent powers of each. We talk sometimes of a great talent for conversation, as if it were a permanent property in some individuals. Conversation is an evanescent relation,—no more. A man is reputed to have thought and eloquence; he cannot, for all that, say a word to his cousin or his uncle. They accuse his silence with as much reason as they would blame the insignificance of a dial in the shade. In the sun it will mark the hour. Among those who enjoy his thought, he will regain his tongue.

Friendship requires that rare mean betwixt likeness and unlikeness, that piques each with the presence of power and of consent in the other party. Let me be alone to the end of the world, rather than that my friend should overstep, by a word or a look, his real sympathy. I am equally balked by antagonism and by compliance. Let him not cease an instant to be himself. The only joy I have in his being mine, is that the not mine is mine. I hate, where I looked for a manly furtherance, or at least a manly resistance, to find a mush of concession. Better be a nettle in the side of your friend than his echo. The condition which high friendship demands is ability to do without it. That high office requires great and sublime parts. There must be very two, before there can be very one.

Let it be an alliance of two large, formidable natures, mutually beheld, mutually feared, before yet they recognize the deep identity which beneath these disparities unites them.

He only is fit for this society who is magnanimous; who is sure that greatness and goodness are always economy; who is not swift to intermeddle with his fortunes. Let him not intermeddle with this. Leave to the diamond its ages to grow, nor expect to accelerate the births of the eternal. Friendship demands a religious treatment. We talk of choosing our friends, but friends are self-elected. Reverence is a great part of it. Treat your friend as a spectacle. Of course, he has merits that are not yours, and that you cannot honour, if you must needs hold him close to your person. Stand aside; give those merits room; let them mount and expand. Are you the friend of your friend's buttons, or of his thought? To a great heart he will still be a stranger in a thousand particulars, that he may come near in the holiest ground. Leave it to girls and boys to regard a friend as property, and to suck a short and all-confounding pleasure, instead of the noblest benefit.

Let us buy our entrance to this guild by a long probation. Why should we desecrate noble and beautiful souls by intruding on them? Why insist on rash personal relations with your friend? Why go to his house, or know his mother and brother and sisters? Why be visited by him at your own? Are these things material to our covenant? Leave this touching and clawing. Let him be to me a spirit. A message, a thought, a sincerity, a glance from him, I want, but not news, nor pottage. I can get politics, and chat, and neighbourly conveniences from cheaper companions. Should not the society of my friend be to me poetic, pure, universal, and great as nature itself? Ought I to feel that our tie is profane in comparison with yonder bar of cloud that sleeps on the horizon, or that clump of waving grass that divides the brook? Let us not vilify, but raise it to that standard. That great, defying eye, that scornful beauty of his mien and action, do not pique yourself on reducing, but rather fortify and enhance. Worship his superiorities; wish him not less by a thought, but hoard and tell them all. Guard him as thy counterpart. Let him be to thee for ever a sort of beautiful enemy, untamable, devoutly revered, and not a trivial conveniency to be soon outgrown and cast aside. The hues of the opal, the light of the diamond, are not to be seen, if the eye is too near. To my friend I write a letter, and from him I receive a letter. That seems to you a little. It suffices me. It is a spiritual gift worthy of him to give, and of me to receive. It profanes nobody. In these warm lines the heart will trust itself, as it will not to the tongue, and pour out the prophecy of a godlier existence than all the annals of heroism have yet made good.

Respect so far the holy laws of this fellowship

as not to prejudice its perfect flower by your impatience for its opening. We must be our own before we can be another's. There is, at least, this satisfaction in crime, according to the Latin proverb,—you can speak to your accomplice on even terms. *Crimen quos inquinat, æquat.* To those whom we admire and love, at first we cannot. Yet the least defect of self-possession vitiates, in my judgment, the entire relation. There can never be deep peace between two spirits, never mutual respect, until, in their dialogue, each stands for the whole world.

What is so great as friendship, let us carry with what grandeur of spirit we can. Let us be silent,—so we may hear the whisper of the gods. Let us not interfere. Who set you to cast about what you should say to the select souls, or how to say any thing to such? No matter how ingenious, no matter how graceful and bland. There are innumerable degrees of folly and wisdom, and for you to say aught is to be frivolous. Wait, and thy heart shall speak. Wait until the necessary and everlasting overpowers you, until day and night avail themselves of your lips. The only reward of virtue is virtue; the only way to have a friend is to be one. You shall not come nearer a man by getting into his house. If unlike, his soul only flees the faster from you, and you shall never catch a true glance of his eye. We see the noble afar off, and they repel us; why should we intrude? Late,— very late—we perceive that no arrangements, no introductions, no consuetudes or habits of society, would be of any avail to establish us in such relations with them as we desire,—but solely the uprise of nature in us to the same degree it is in them; then shall we meet as water with water; and if we should not meet them then, we shall not want them, for we are already they. In the last analysis, love is only the reflection of a man's own worthiness from other men. Men have sometimes exchanged names with their friends, as if they would signify that in their friend each loved his own soul.

The higher the style we demand of friendship, of course the less easy to establish it with flesh and blood. We walk alone in the world. Friends, such as we desire, are dreams and fables. But a sublime hope cheers ever the faithful heart, that elsewhere, in other regions of the universal power, souls are now acting, enduring, and daring, which can love us, and which we can love. We may congratulate ourselves that the period of nonage, of follies, of blunders, and of shame, is passed in solitude, and when we are finished men, we shall grasp heroic hands in heroic hands. Only be admonished by what you already see, not to strike leagues of friendship with cheap persons, where no friendship can be. Our impatience betrays us into rash and foolish alliances which no god attends. By persisting in your path, though you forfeit the little you gain the great. You demonstrate yourself, so as to put yourself out of the reach of false relations, and you draw to you the first-born of the world,—those rare pilgrims whereof only one or two wander in nature at once, and before whom the vulgar great show as spectres and shadows merely.

It is foolish to be afraid of making our ties too spiritual, as if so we could lose any genuine love. Whatever correction of our popular views we make from insight, nature will be sure to bear us out in, and though it seem to rob us of some joy, will repay us with a greater. Let us feel, if we will, the absolute insulation of man. We are sure that we have all in us. We go to Europe, or we pursue persons, or we read books, in the instinctive faith that these will call it out and reveal us to ourselves. Beggars all. The persons are such as we; the Europe, an old faded garment of dead persons; the books their ghosts. Let us drop this idolatry. Let us give over this mendicancy. Let us even bid our dearest friends farewell, and defy them, saying 'Who are you? Unhand me: I will be dependent no more.' Ah! seest thou not, O brother, that thus we part only to meet again on a higher platform, and only be more each other's, because we are more our own? A friend is Janus-faced; he looks to the past and the future. He is the child of all my foregoing hours, the prophet of those to come, and the harbinger of a greater friend.

I do then with my friends as I do with my books. I would have them where I can find them, but I seldom use them. We must have society on our own terms, and admit or exclude it on the slightest cause. I cannot afford to speak much with my friend. If he is great, he makes me so great that I cannot descend to converse. In the great days, presentiments hover before me in the firmament. I ought then to dedicate myself to them. I go in that I may seize them, I go out that I may seize them. I fear only that I may lose them receding into the sky in which now they are only a patch of brighter light. Then, though I prize my friends, I cannot afford to talk with them and study their visions, lest I lose my own. It would indeed give me a certain household joy to quit this lofty seeking, this spiritual astronomy, or search of stars, and come down to warm sympathies with you; but then, I know well I shall mourn always the vanishing of my mighty gods. It is true, next week I shall have languid moods, when I can well afford to occupy myself with foreign objects; then I shall regret the lost literature of your mind, and wish you were by my side again. But if you come, perhaps you will fill my mind only with new visions, not with yourself but with your lustres, and I shall not be able any more than now to converse with you. So I will owe to my friends this evanescent intercourse. I will receive from them, not what they have, but what they are. They shall give me that which properly they cannot give, but which emanates from them. But they shall not hold me by any relations less subtle and pure. We will meet as though we met not, and part as though we parted not.

It has seemed to me lately more possible than I knew, to carry a friendship greatly on one side, without due correspondence on the other. Why should I cumber myself with regrets that the receiver is not capacious? It never troubles the sun that some of his rays fall wide and vain into ungrateful space, and only a small part on the reflecting planet. Let your greatness educate the crude and cold companion. If he is unequal, he will presently pass away; but thou art enlarged by thy own shining, and, no longer a mate for frogs and worms, dost soar and burn with the gods of the empyrean. It is thought a disgrace to love unrequited. But the great will see that true love cannot be unrequited. True love transcends the unworthy object, and dwells and broods on the eternal, and when the poor interposed mask crumbles, it is not sad, but feels rid of so much earth, and feels its independency the surer. Yet these things may hardly be said without a sort of treachery to the relation. The essence of friendship is entireness, a total magnanimity and trust. It must not surmise or provide for infirmity. It treats its object as a god, that it may deify both.

BERTRAND RUSSELL
Machines and the Emotions

Will machines destroy emotions, or will emotions destroy machines? This question was suggested long ago by Samuel Butler in *Erewhon*, but it is growing more and more actual as the empire of machinery is enlarged.

At first sight, it is not obvious why there should be any opposition between machines and emotions. Every normal boy loves machines; the bigger and more powerful they are, the more he loves them. Nations which have a long tradition of artistic excellence, like the Japanese, are captivated by Western mechanical methods as soon as they come across them, and long only to imitate us as quickly as possible. Nothing annoys an educated and travelled Asiatic so much as to hear praise of "the wisdom of the East" or the traditional virtues of Asiatic civilization. He feels as a boy would feel who was told to play with dolls instead of toy automobiles. And like a boy, he would prefer a real automobile to a toy one, not realizing that it may run over him.

In the West, when machinery was new, there was the same delight in it, except on the part of a few poets and æsthetes. The nineteenth century considered itself superior to its predecessors chiefly because of its mechanical progress. Peacock, in its early years, makes fun of the "steam intellect society," because he is a literary man, to whom the Greek and Latin authors represent civilization; but he is conscious of being out of touch with the prevailing tendencies of his time. Rousseau's disciples with the return to Nature, the Lake Poets with their mediævalism, William Morris with his *News from Nowhere* (a country where it is always June and everybody is engaged in haymaking), all represent a purely sentimental and essentially reactionary opposition to machinery. Samuel Butler was the first man to apprehend intellectually the non-sentimental case against machines, but in him it may have been no more than a *jeu d'esprit*—certainly it was not a deeply held conviction. Since his day numbers of people in the most mechanized nations have been tending to adopt in earnest a view similar to that of the Erewhonians; this view, that is to say, has been latent or explicit in the attitude of many rebels against existing industrial methods.

Machines are worshipped because they are beautiful, and valued because they confer power; they are hated because they are hideous, and loathed because they impose slavery. Do not let us suppose that one of these attitudes is "right" and the other "wrong," any more than it would be right to maintain that men have heads but wrong to maintain that they have feet, though we can easily imagine Lilliputians disputing this question concerning Gulliver. A machine is like a Djinn in the Arabian Nights: beautiful and beneficent to its master, but hideous and terrible to his enemies. But in our day nothing is allowed to show itself with such naked simplicity. The master of the machine, it is true, lives at a distance from it, where he cannot hear its noise or see its unsightly heaps of slag or smell its noxious fumes; if he ever sees it, the occasion is before it is installed in use, when he can admire its force or its delicate precision without being troubled by dust and heat. But when he is challenged to consider the machine from the point of view of those who have to live with it and work it, he has a ready answer. He can point out that, owing to its operations, these men can purchase more goods—often vastly more—than their great-grandfathers could. It follows that they must be happier than their great-grandfathers—if we are to accept an assumption which is made by almost every one.

The assumption is, that the possession of material commodities is what makes men happy. It is thought that a man who has two rooms and two beds and two loaves must be twice as happy as a man who has one room and one bed and one loaf. In a word, it is thought that happiness is proportional to income. A few people, not always quite sincerely, challenge this idea in the name of religion or morality; but they are glad if they increase their income by the eloquence of their preaching. It is not from a moral or religious point of view that I wish to challenge it; it is from the point of view of psychology and observation of life. If happiness is proportional to income, the case for machinery is unanswerable; if not, the whole question remains to be examined.

Men have physical needs, and they have emotions. While physical needs are unsatisfied, they take first place; but when they are satisfied, emotions unconnected with them become important in deciding whether a man is to be happy or unhappy. In modern industrial communities there are many men, women, and children whose bare physical needs are not adequately supplied; as regards them, I do not deny that the first requisite for happiness is an increase of income. But they are a minority, and it would not be difficult to give the bare necessaries of life to all of them. It is not of them that I wish to speak, but of those who have more than is necessary to support existence—not only those who have much more, but also those who have only a little more.

Why do we, in fact, almost all of us, desire to increase our incomes? It may seem, at first sight, as though material goods were what we desire. But, in fact, we desire these mainly in order to impress our neighbours. When a man moves into a larger house in a more genteel quarter, he reflects that "better" people will call on his wife, and some unprosperous cronies of former days can be dropped. When he sends his son to a good school or an expensive university, he consoles himself for the heavy fees by thoughts of the social kudos to be gained. In every big city, whether of Europe or of America, houses in some districts are more expensive than equally good houses in other districts, merely because they are more fashionable. One of the most powerful of all our passions is the desire to be admired and respected. As things stand, admiration and respect are given to the man who seems to be rich. This is the chief reason why people wish to be rich. The actual goods purchased by their money play quite a secondary part. Take, for example, a millionaire who cannot tell one picture from another, but has acquired a gallery of old masters by the help of experts. The only pleasure he derives from his pictures is the thought that others know how much they have cost; he would derive more direct enjoyment from sentimental chromos out of Christmas numbers, but he would not obtain the same satisfaction for his vanity.

All this might be different, and has been different in many societies. In aristocratic epochs, men have been admired for their birth. In some circles in Paris, men are admired for their artistic or literary excellence, strange as it may seem. In a German university, a man may actually be admired for his learning. In India saints are admired; in China, sages. The study of these differing societies shows the correctness of our analysis, for in all of them we find a large percentage of men who are indifferent to money so long as they have enough to keep alive on, but are keenly desirous of the merits by which, in their environment, respect is to be won.

The importance of these facts lies in this, that the modern desire for wealth is not inherent in human nature, and could be destroyed by different social institutions. If, by law, we all had exactly the same income, we should have to seek some other way of being superior to our neighbours, and most of our present craving for material possessions would cease. Moreover, since this craving is in the nature of a competition, it only brings happiness when we outdistance a rival, to whom it brings correlative pain. A general increase of wealth gives no competitive advantage, and therefore brings no competitive happiness. There is, of course, *some* pleasure derived from the actual enjoyment of goods purchased, but, as we have seen, this is a very small part of what makes us desire wealth. And in so far as our desire is competitive, no increase of human happiness as a whole comes from increase of wealth, whether general or particular.

If we are to argue that machinery increases happiness, therefore, the increase of material prosperity which it brings cannot weigh very heavily in its favour, except in so far as it may be used to prevent absolute destitution. But there is no inherent reason why it should be so used. Destitution can be prevented without machinery where the population is stationary; of this France may serve as an example, since there is very little destitution and much less machinery than in America, England, or pre-war Germany. Conversely, there may be much destitution where there is much machinery; of this we have examples in the industrial areas of England a hundred years ago and of Japan at the present day. The prevention of destitution does not depend upon machines, but upon quite other factors—partly density of population, and partly political conditions. And apart from prevention of destitution, the value of increasing wealth is not very great.

Meanwhile, machines deprive us of two things which are certainly important ingredients of human happiness, namely, spontaneity and variety. Machines have their own pace, and their own insistent demands: a man who has an expensive plant must keep it working. The great trouble with the machine, from the point of view of the emotions, is its *regularity*. And, of course, conversely, the great objection to the emotions, from the point of view of the machine, is their *irregularity*. As the machine dominates the thoughts of people who consider themselves "serious," the highest praise they can give to a man is to suggest that he has the qualities of a machine—that he is reliable, punctual, exact, etc. And an "irregular" life has come to be synonymous with a bad life. Against this point of view Bergson's philosophy was a protest—not, to my mind, wholly sound from an intellectual point of view, but inspired by a wholesome dread of seeing men turned more and more into machines.

In life, as opposed to thought, the rebellion of our instincts against enslavement to mechanism has hitherto taken a most unfortunate direction. The impulse to war has always existed since men took to living in societies, but it did not, in the past, have the same intensity or virulence as it has in our day. In the eighteenth century, England and France had innumerable wars, and contended for the hegemony of the world; but they liked and respected each other the whole time. Officer prisoners joined in the social life of their captors, and were honoured guests at their dinner-parties. At the beginning of our war with Holland in 1665, a man came home from Africa with atrocity stories about the Dutch there; we [the British] persuaded ourselves that his story was false, punished him, and published the Dutch denial. In the late war we should have knighted him, and imprisoned anyone who threw doubt on his veracity. The greater ferocity of modern war is attributable to machines, which operate in three different ways. First, they make it possible to have larger armies. Secondly, they facilitate a cheap Press, which flourishes by appealing to men's baser passions. Thirdly—and this is the point that concerns us—they starve the anarchic, spontaneous side of human nature, which works underground, producing an obscure discontent, to which the thought of war appeals as affording possible relief. It is a mistake to attribute a vast upheaval like the late war merely to the machinations of politicians. In Russia, perhaps, such an explanation would have been adequate; that is one reason why Russia fought halfheartedly, and made a revolution to secure peace. But in England, Germany, and the United States (in 1917), no Government could have withstood the popular demand for war. A popular demand of this sort must have an instinctive basis, and for my part I believe that the modern increase in warlike instinct is attributable to the dissatisfaction (mostly unconscious) caused by the regularity, monotony, and tameness of modern life.

It is obvious that we cannot deal with this situation by abolishing machinery. Such a measure would be reactionary, and is in any case impracticable. The only way of avoiding the evils at present associated with machinery is to provide breaks in the monotony, with every encouragement to high adventure during the intervals. Many men would cease to desire war if they had opportunities to risk their lives in Alpine climbing; one of the ablest and most vigorous workers for peace that it has been my good fortune to know habitually spent his summer climbing the most dangerous peaks in the Alps. If every working man had a month in the year during which, if he chose, he could be taught to work an aeroplane, or encouraged to hunt for sapphires in the Sahara, or otherwise enabled to engage in some dangerous and exciting pursuit involving quick personal initiative, the popular love of war would become confined to women and invalids. I confess I know no method of making these classes pacific, but I am convinced that a scientific psychology would find a method if it undertook the task in earnest.

Machines have altered our way of life, but not our instincts. Consequently there is maladjustment. The whole psychology of the emotions and instincts is as yet in its infancy; a beginning has been made by psycho-analysis, but only a beginning. What we may accept from psycho-analysis is the fact that people will, in action, pursue various ends which they do not *consciously* desire, and will have an attendant set of quite irrational beliefs which enable them to pursue these ends without knowing that they are doing so. But orthodox psycho-analysis has unduly simplified our unconscious purposes, which are numerous, and differ from one person to another. It is to be hoped that social and political phenomena will soon come to be understood from this point of view, and will thus throw light on average human nature.

Moral self-control, and external prohibition of harmful acts, are not adequate methods of dealing with our anarchic instincts. The reason they are inadequate is that these instincts are capable of as many disguises as the Devil in mediæval legend, and some of these disguises deceive even the elect. The only adequate method is to discover what are the needs of our instinctive nature, and then to search for the least harmful way of satisfying them. Since spontaneity is what is most thwarted by machines, the only thing that can be *provided* is opportunity; the use made of opportunity must be left to the initiative of the individual. No doubt considerable expense would be involved; but it would not be comparable to the expense of war. Understanding of human nature must be the basis of any real improvement in human life. Science has done wonders in mastering the laws of the physical world, but our own nature is much less understood, as yet, than the nature of stars and electrons. When science learns to understand human nature, it will be able to bring a happiness into our lives which machines and the physical sciences have failed to create.

VIRGINIA WOOLF
On the Value of Laughter

The old idea was that comedy represented the failings of human nature, and that tragedy pictured men as greater than they are. To paint them truly one must, it seems, strike a mean between the two, and the result is something too serious to be comic, too imperfect to be tragic, and this we may call humour. Humour, we have been told, is denied to women. They may be tragic or comic, but the particular blend which makes a humorist is to be found only in men. But experiments are dangerous things, and in trying to attain the humorist's point of view – in balancing himself on that pinnacle which is denied his sisters – the male gymnast not infrequently topples over ignominiously on to the other side, and either plunges headlong into buffoonery or else descends to the hard ground of serious commonplace, where, to do him justice, he is entirely at his ease. It may be that tragedy – a necessary ingredient – is not so common as it was in the time of Shakespeare, and therefore the present age has had to provide a decorous substitute which dispenses with blood and daggers, and looks its best in a chimney-pot hat and long frock-coat. This we may call the spirit of solemnity, and if spirits have a gender, there is no doubt that it is masculine. Now, comedy is of the sex of the graces and the muses, and when this solemn gentleman advances to offer his compliments she looks and laughs, and looks again till irresistible laughter comes over her, and she flies to hide her merriment in the bosoms of her sisters. Thus humour very rarely comes into the world, and comedy has a hard fight for it. Pure laughter, such as we hear on the lips of children and silly women, is in disrepute. It is held to be the voice of folly and frivolity inspired neither by knowledge nor emotion. It gives no message, conveys no information; it is an inarticulate utterance like the bark of a dog or the bleat of sheep, and it is beneath the dignity of a race that has made itself a language to express itself thus.

But there are some things that are beyond words and not beneath them, and laughter is one of these. For laughter is the one sound, inarticulate though it be, that no animal can produce. If the dog on the hearthrug groans in pain or barks for joy we recognise his meaning and it has nothing strange in it, but suppose he were to laugh? Suppose that when you came into the room he did not express his legitimate joy at the sight of you by tail or tongue, but burst into peals of laughter – grinned – shook his sides and showed all the usual signs of extreme amusement. Your feeling then would be one of shrinking and horror, as though a human voice had spoken from a beast's mouth. Nor can we imagine that beings in a higher state than ourselves laugh; laughter seems to belong essentially and exclusively to men and women. Laughter is the expression of the comic spirit within us, and the comic spirit concerns itself with oddities and eccentricities and deviations from the recognised pattern. It makes its comment in the sudden and spontaneous laugh which comes, we hardly know why, and we cannot tell when. If we took time to think – to analyse this impression that the comic spirit registers – we should find, doubtless, that what is superficially comic is fundamentally tragic, and while the smile was on our lips the water would stand in our eyes. This – the words are Bunyan's – has been accepted as a definition of humour; but the laughter of comedy has no burden of tears. At the same time, though its office is comparatively slight compared with that of true humour, the value of laughter in life and in art cannot be over-rated. Humour is of the heights; the rarest minds alone can climb the pinnacle whence the whole of life can be viewed as in a panorama; but comedy walks the highways and reflects the trivial and accidental – the venial faults and peculiarities of all who pass in its bright little mirror. Laughter more than anything else preserves our sense of proportion; it is for ever reminding us that we are but human, that no man is quite a hero or entirely a villain. Directly we forget to laugh we see things out of proportion and lose our sense of reality. Dogs, mercifully, cannot laugh, because, if they could, they would realise the terrible limitations of being a dog. Men and women are just high enough in the scale of civilisation to be intrusted with the power of knowing their own failings and have been granted the gift of laughing at them. But we are in danger of losing this precious privilege, or of crushing it out of our breasts, by a mass of crude and ponderous knowledge.

To be able to laugh at a person you must, to begin with, be able to see him as he is. All his cloak of wealth and rank and learning, so far as it is a superficial accumulation, must not blunt the keen blade of the comic spirit which probes to the quick. It is a commonplace that children have a surer power of knowing men for what they are than grown people, and I believe that the verdict that women pass upon character will not be revoked at the Day of Judgment. Women and children, then, are the chief ministers of the comic spirit, because their eyes are not clouded with learning nor are their brains choked with the theories of books, so that men and things still preserve their original sharp outlines. All the hideous excrescences that have overgrown our modern life, the pomps and conventions and dreary solemnities, dread nothing so much as the flash of laughter which, like lightning, shrivels them up and leaves the bones bare. It is because their laughter possesses this quality that children are feared by people who are conscious of affectations and unrealities; and it is probably for this reason that women are looked upon with such disfavour in the learned professions. The danger is that they may laugh, like the child in Hans Andersen who said that the king went naked when his elders worshipped the splendid raiment that did not exist. In art, as in life, all the worst blunders arise from a lack of proportion, and the tendency of both is to be over-emphatically serious. Our great writers blossom in purple and roll in magnificent periods; our lesser writers multiply their adjectives and luxuriate in the sentimentalism which in a lower class produces the sensational placard and the melodrama. We go to funerals and to sick-beds far more willingly than to marriages and festivals, and we cannot rid our minds of the belief that there is something virtuous in tears and that black is the most becoming habit. There is nothing, indeed, so difficult as laughter, but no quality is more valuable. It is a knife that both prunes and trains and gives symmetry and sincerity to our acts and to the spoken and the written word.

Permissions Acknowledgements

'Reading' by Rose Macaulay reproduced by permission of The Society of Authors as the literary representative of the Estate of Rose Macaulay.

'Machines and the Emotions' reproduced from *Sceptical Essays*, 2nd Edition (Routledge Classics) by Bertrand Russell, published by Routledge. © 1996 The Bertrand Russell Peace Foundation Ltd, reproduced by arrangement with Taylor & Francis Group.

MACMILLAN COLLECTOR'S LIBRARY

Own the world's great works of literature in one beautiful collectible library

Designed and curated to appeal to book lovers everywhere, Macmillan Collector's Library editions are small enough to travel with you and striking enough to take pride of place on your bookshelf. These much-loved literary classics also make the perfect gift.

Beautifully made, every Macmillan Collector's Library book adheres to the same high production values. Each hardback features gilt edges, a ribbon marker and cloth binding, and every paperback has a bespoke illustrated cover.

Discover a new and exciting anthology or cherish your favourite classic stories with this elegant collection.

Macmillan Collector's Library: own, collect, and treasure

Discover the full range at
panmacmillan.com/mcl